100+ ACTIVITIES
FOR
HOUSTON KIDS

BY MEGAN F. SALCH

D1368537

Dedication
To the Frazier and Salch families,
who continue to give all they have to nurture their Houston children.
Thanks for the memories.

I have selected the activities in this book based upon my family's experiences with these organizations. This is not an exhaustive list of available activities and omission of an activity does not necessarily imply the activity is not worthwhile. Individual preferences may vary and, thus, this book is intended to offer ideas for activities, not assurances that an activity will be perfect for any particular child. It is not a substitute for the individual judgment or exercise of responsible supervision by a parent or guardian.

ISBN-13: 978-0-9788823-0-3
ISBN-10: 0-9788823-0-X

Book cover and illustrations by Debbie Rohde and Robbie Short.
Book layout by Fred Bobovnyk Jr.
Edited by Roger Leslie.

ATTENTION PARENTS, GRANDPARENTS AND CAREGIVERS!

There are so many fun activities to do in Houston, but who has time to research them all? Welcome to *100+ Activities for Houston Kids* — an easy way for families to have fun together. Throw boredom out the window. The 2007 edition of this guidebook is organized to help your family find great activities quickly.

Chapter 1 lists seasonal activities throughout greater Houston. Some activities occur on a specific date each year, while others run through an entire month. So your family can use this guidebook year after year, I have not listed specific dates. Instead, you'll find the usual month in which each activity takes place. Exact dates for each year can be located at **www.TellYourTale.com/kids**.

Chapter 2 highlights venues that welcome families all year long without any seasonal requirements. This listing is a good supplement to the calendar of events provided in the previous chapter.

Each listing in chapters 1 and 2 includes a:
- category or type of activity (more than one may apply)
- description
- recommended age
- admission price
- time
- physical location
- web site and/or phone number for more details
- two grade boxes that allow a parent and a child to evaluate the activity based on letter grades given in school

Art & Music

Charity/ Volunteer

History

Holiday

Nature

Parade

Science

Sports

Throughout the book, the days of the week are abbreviated as follows:

Monday: M
Tuesday: T
Wednesday: W
Thursday: Th
Friday: F
Saturday: Sat
Sunday: Sun

Chapter 3 features family-friendly restaurants. You no longer need to give up tasty food for a kid-friendly atmosphere. Chapter 3 helps you navigate Houston eateries by highlighting FREE kid nights or family specials as well as restaurants that truly welcome families by offering kids' menus, games or play equipment, and more.

It's important to note that our family and friends have visited every activity and restaurant in this guidebook. We offer personal insight and tips for making family time enjoyable and memorable. This is valuable information you won't find in other resources.

I've made every effort to publish correct information on each activity, but dates, times and prices are subject to change. Call the organization to confirm the details before heading to your destination. For regular updates, visit my Web blog at **http://kidsactivityqueen.blogspot.com/**, where several times each week I post information on new openings, discounts, and recent announcements. I also invite you to subscribe to my FREE monthly newsletter. Subscribing takes only two minutes so visit my Web site at **www.TellYourTale.com/kids** to sign up today.

I hope this guidebook brings you and the children in your lives together through positive experiences. Take time today to plan your next activity and talk about what you enjoyed most. Play it month to month or skim through this guidebook to find events that interest you and your children. Then, unleash the good times!

Hope to see you and your family around Houston!

Megan F. Salch
"The Kids Activity Queen"

CONTENTS

CHAPTER 1: SEASONAL ACTIVITIES FOR HOUSTON KIDS

January:

The **Houston Rockets** basketball team hosts kids' night in January to celebrate the birthday of team mascot Clutch. Visiting NBA mascots from across the country perform at halftime. Plus, children often receive fan giveaways.

Recommended age: 3+ years
Admission: Tickets range from $10 – $185
Time: varies each year
Physical location: Toyota Center at 1510 Polk Street in downtown Houston
www.Rockets.com
Buy tickets at 866-4HOUTIX (866-446-8849), **www.ToyotaCenterTix.com** or participating Randalls stores.

How would you rate this? ☐ ☐

The third Monday in January is **Martin Luther King, Jr. Day**. The Houston Zoo celebrates by offering free admittance all day! Grab a coat and enjoy the animals when it's not so hot in town.

Recommended age: 1+ years
Admission: None today
Time: 9 am-5 pm
Physical location: 1513 N. MacGregor
www.HoustonZoo.org 713-533-6500

How would you rate this? ☐ ☐

Be sure to take advantage of the **Mardi Gras** parades in Galveston. These are fun for the whole family as kids of all ages love seeing the festive floats and costumes. Get in on the action by catching beads, cups and more. All parades are publicly accessible. Bring strollers or wagons for young children. Here are three kid-friendly parades in Galveston to check out. Happy Mardi Gras!

— **The Krewe of Aquarius** typically holds its parade on the seawall from 14th Street to 57th Street. This is a great parade during the day for the entire family. You might even catch stuffed animals, frisbees and candy.

— **The Krewe of Barkus and Meoux Mardi Gras Parade** (Parade of the Animals) is super fun. Families bring all types of pets from cats and dogs to ferrets and iguanas. The parade route varies each year.

— **The Mardi Gras Children's Parade** often follows the same route as the Parade of the Animals and is a great follow-up for kids. It includes familiar cartoon animals and giveaways range from beads to stuffed animals and kid-sized cups.

Recommended age: All ages.
Admission: No fee to attend the parades but paid admission onto The Strand may apply
www.MardiGrasGalveston.com
888-GAL-ISLE (888-425-4753)

How would you rate this? ☐ ☐

2/14: Happy Valentine's Day. Love your kids at the **Valentine Skate** for kids 7 and younger. The Dairy Ashford Roller Rink holds this event as good, clean fun. Bring your child's tricycle or stroller if he/she is too young to skate. The rink also pumps up the fun by throwing a few balls onto the skate area. My 10-month-old absolutely loved this. Enjoy preschool tunes like the "Hokey Pokey." Plus, each child receives candy and a skating coupon for a future visit.

Dairy Ashford Roller Rink
Recommended age: 0-7 years
Admission: $6
Time: 10 am-1 pm
Physical location: 1820 S Dairy Ashford St.
www.SkateDARR.com 281-493-5651

How would you rate this?

February in Houston means it's time for the downtown **Rodeo Parade**. Chuck wagons, horses, and real cowboys and cowgirls have trotted their way to this rodeo for more than 65 years. This is a wonderful experience for the kids in your family to see cows, horses, cowboys and cowgirls. Dress up in your favorite denim and head downtown, but bring a blanket and jackets for the little ones since it's often cool outside this time of year. Head toward the beginning of the parade route to see parade participants before they tire.
Recommended age: All
Admission: No charge to watch the parade but parking fees may apply

Time: varies each year but usually begins mid-morning
Physical location: downtown Houston
www.hlsr.com/Parade 832-667-1000

How would you rate this? ☐ ☐

The Houston Livestock Show and Rodeo
in February and March is like no other rodeo
nationwide. Matinee performances offer children a
chance to see bull riders, barrel racers and famous
performers ranging in music style from country to
rock. But there's so much more than the rodeo
itself. This is a great family activity. The outdoor
carnival presents fun rides, games and tasty treats.
Destination: AGventure is an educational
exhibit about… you guessed it… agriculture. Our
daughter and nephew enjoyed collecting cards at
each exhibit to receive a prize at the end. Don't
forget the petting zoo that features chickens, goats,
ducks and much more. Rodeo visitors can also view
art work from local students with real talent. The
pig races and pony rides are wonderful treasures,
too.
Recommended age: All
Admission: Rodeo performance tickets begin at $17.
The FunPass! costs $20 and gives you access to
everything except the rodeo/concert activities for all 20
days of rodeo.
Time: 9 am-9 pm
Physical location: Reliant Stadium and Reliant Park at 1
Reliant Park
www.hlsr.com 832-667-1000

How would you rate this? ☐ ☐

March:

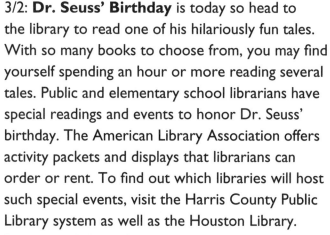

3/2: **Dr. Seuss' Birthday** is today so head to the library to read one of his hilariously fun tales. With so many books to choose from, you may find yourself spending an hour or more reading several tales. Public and elementary school librarians have special readings and events to honor Dr. Seuss' birthday. The American Library Association offers activity packets and displays that librarians can order or rent. To find out which libraries will host such special events, visit the Harris County Public Library system as well as the Houston Library.

Recommended age: 1+ years

Admission: None

Time: 9 am-6 pm

Physical location: various

www.HoustonLibrary.org www.hcpl.lib.tx.us

832-393-1313

How would you rate this?

On the third Saturday of each month, March through November, the members of the Houston Area Live Steamers offer **FREE train rides** to the public. They have two club diesel engines that normally run the passenger trains but many times you will find a steam engine also running. They also have specially designed cars for the young and the young at heart who enjoy hearing the clickety-clack of the rails.

Recommended age: All

Admission: FREE

Time: 10 am-4 pm
Physical location: 17802 Roberts Rd. in Hockley (Take 290 north to Roberts Rd. from central Houston.)
www.HALS.org/index.html or
email **nfo206@HALS.org**

How would you rate this?

3/17: Wishing you the luck of the Irish! Get dressed in green for Houston's **Saint Patrick's Day Parade**. With no admission cost, this is entertainment for family and friends. Bring a wagon for youngsters to sit in.
Recommended age: All
Admission: No charge to watch parade but parking fees may apply
Time: varies each year
Physical location: downtown Houston
www.PublicWorks.CityOfHouston.gov/ Traffic/Events.htm

How would you rate this?

The **Bayou City Art Festival** has been rated one of the top 200 events in the United States. Don't miss this annual event, occurring in March. (The festival is also held in downtown in October.) Enjoy the park's beauty while mingling with 300+ artists from across the nation. Kids' activities include hat painting, sand blasting, jewelry making and more. This is a rain or shine event. Sunday is an especially family-friendly day for this event.
Recommended age: 1+ years

Admission: Adults $8; Children under 12 free.
Time: 10 am-6 pm
Physical location: Memorial Park in central Houston (5 miles from downtown)
www.BayouCityArtFestival.com 713-521-0133

How would you rate this? ☐ ☐

Designated as "Houston's Official Family Celebration," the **H-E-B Houston Children's Festival** presents 10 adventure zones, six entertainment stages and more. The festival usually occurs toward the end of March or beginning of April each year. The 2006 event drew 50,000 visitors so this is a BIG event. Proceeds benefit Child Advocates, Inc. and the abused and neglected children that it serves. We found the Sunday crowd to be much more family-oriented as people attended after church.

Recommended age: 2+ years
Admission: $6 per person with one H-E-B grocery receipt for each ticket; $8 at the gate without an H-E-B grocery receipt; Children under age 3 are FREE
Time: 10:30 am-6:30 pm
Physical location: downtown Houston's theatre district
www.HoustonChildrensFestival.com

How would you rate this? ☐ ☐

4/1: April Fools Day is an excuse for pulling pranks. Take a trip to one of Houston's **parks** and just fool around. The weather in April tends to be nice so pack a lunch and enjoy a picnic. For a list of city parks with a map, visit **www.HoustonTx.gov/Parks**.

Recommended age: All
Admission: FREE
Time: Dawn to dusk
Physical location: various locations throughout Houston
www.HoustonTx.gov/Parks 713-845-1000

How would you rate this?

The **Grand Kid's Festival** is a fantastic way for parents and grandparents to spend time with their young children in April. Families enjoy three blocks of downtown Galveston festivities. Plus, The Grand's musical productions are performed throughout the festival. The crowd is manageable and family-oriented, yet another benefit of this annual favorite.

Recommended age: 1+ years
Admission: $8 - $10
Time: 10 am-5 pm
Physical location: 2020 Postoffice Street in Galveston
www.TheGrand.com

409-765-1894 or 800-821-1894

How would you rate this?

Take me out to the ballgame. This month kicks off baseball season. **Minute Maid Park** is a wonder to see and offers something for everyone. Arrive early to take advantage of giveaways on special game days. Watch the retractable roof on this ballpark, and cheer on the Astros as the train sounds its horn when the Astros score. Join the Coca-Cola Astros Buddies Club for $10 per year and maximize your Astros spirit with special Astros Buddies game days and Astros garb. Go 'Stros!

Hungry? Head to CHEW CHEW EXPRESS (Sections 133 & 416), which provides smaller meals for younger fans. Squeeze Play is located on the northeast corner of the ballpark at the Right Field Entrance near Section 133. Young fans, accompanied by an adult, can test their speed with an interactive Squeeze Play game or their hitting prowess in the Splatting Cage. To cool off, fans can indulge in delicious slushies at the Minute Maid juice bar. With the availability of picnic tables and several TV screens, this is the perfect place for the whole family to enjoy a day at Minute Maid Park. Look for Junction Jack, the Astros mascot, who loyally attends every game.

Fans age two and under may be admitted to Astros games without an admission ticket. However, they must sit in the lap of an accompanying adult. Sixteen family restrooms are available throughout the ballpark so, yes, Daddy can change the diaper or take the little tikes to the bathroom!
Recommended age: 1 + years

Admission: $1+ for children; $5+ for adults
Time: 1 pm, 3 pm, 6 pm and 7 pm game times
Physical location: 501 Crawford Street in downtown Houston
www.Astros.com/Kids 713-259-8978

How would you rate this?

The Woodlands Waterway Arts Festival
includes booths with approximately 200 local and
regional artists. Stroll the 1.25-mile paved walkway
to see what different artists have to offer. The
2006 event expected 15,000 people. This is a rain
or shine event usually held in April.

Recommended age: 3+ years
Admission: Adults $8; Children under 12 FREE.
*Time: Hours vary throughout the weekend but are
usually 10 am–5 pm*
*Physical location: alongside the waterway through The
Woodlands Town Center from The Marriott Waterway
Hotel and Convention Center alongside The Cynthia
Woods Mitchell Pavilion culminating at the four-acre
Town Green Park*
www.BayouCityArtFestival.com 713-521-0133

How would you rate this?

Each April, the **SPCA's Mutt Strut** allows
children to learn about pets without adopting them
all. This annual walk is held downtown and raises
money for animal cruelty prevention. Registrations
and pledges may be turned in the morning of the
event so that your family and pet can participate in

the short walk downtown. Alternatively, just head to Fish Plaza to watch all the animals in the walk. Your kids will love the parade-like feel. Then, enjoy the post-walk activities for all animal lovers. The What a Mutt Contest is quite entertaining. If you bring your pet, please be sure he/she is on a leash.
Recommended age: All
Admission: None but registration in the walk is $35 per person.
Time: The walk begins around 10:30 am. Post-walk fun continues until 3 pm.
Physical location: Fish Plaza in front of Wortham Plaza on Prairie and Smith downtown
www.SPCAHouston.org 713-869-SPCA (7722)

How would you rate this?

Galveston's **Grand 1894 Opera House** produces educational and entertaining theatrical performances for young children. Many of the productions are based on popular children's books so kids easily identify with the well-known characters. Performances range from Disney specials to the tales of the Berenstain Bears.
Recommended age: 3+ years
Admission: $8 - $10
Time: 10 am and noon performances
Physical location: 2020 Postoffice Street in Galveston
www.TheGrand.com
409-765-1894 or 800-821-1894

How would you rate this?

The **Grand Prix of Houston** is an exhilarating experience for kids and adults. (Go, Pinky! I choose my favorite cars based on car color or how nice the drivers were in interviews. My sister-in-law chooses drivers based on statistics and previous finishes.) Your family can attend the day activities to see race cars in action. The actual races are at night and best reserved for teens and adults. However, I was pleasantly surprised to see so many kids enjoying the festivities in 2006. In addition to rooting on your favorite cars, there's off-track entertainment for the youngsters. The Family Fun Zone includes a ferris wheel, bungee trampoline, mechanical bull, micro reality race cars, a giant slide, the elephant belly bouncer, face painters, jugglers and balloon artists. Buy some ear plugs from your local drug store because the race cars are incredibly loud.

Recommended age: 6+ years

Admission: General admission grounds passes start at $10; Reserved tickets usually range $87-$129 for a 3-day ticket.

Time: Gates open between 10 and 11 am each day with practices and qualifying. The actual races are typically in the evening.

Physical location: Reliant Park at 1 Reliant Park, near 610 and Fannin

www.GrandPrixOfHouston.com 713-629-3700

How would you rate this?   ❏   ❏

4/22 is **Earth Day**. Reduce, Reuse, Recycle at the Children's Museum of Houston. Celebrate Earth Day by reusing and conserving natural resources. Did you know that the average person throws away about four pounds of trash each day? Find out what happens to your trash and decide what materials will decompose in a landfill. Learn what you can do to help save the Earth.

Recommended age: 2+ years
Admission: $5; Th 5-8 pm are FREE;
$3 T – Sun 3-5 pm
Time: M-F 9 am-5 pm with extended hours until
8 pm on Th; Sun noon-5 pm
Physical location: 1500 Binz in the Museum District
www.CMHouston.org 713-522-1138

How would you rate this?

Texas celebrates **Arbor Day** on the last Friday in April. The city of Houston has honored this day for more than 20 years. Plant a tree in your yard or help your neighborhood care for its trees in local parks. If you join The Arbor Day Foundation, you will receive 10 trees to plant in your yard. See the Web site below for details. What a wonderful way to participate in nature and discuss the importance of growing and caring for trees. The Arbor Day Web site is full of great ideas.

Recommended age: 1+ years
Admission: FREE
Time: Dawn to dusk
Physical locations: various
www.ArborDay.org

How would you rate this?

We love a good burger but where do all those ingredients come from? Learn just that at **Dewberry Farm** this month at **Hamburger Making**. Kids learn how the ingredients for a perfect burger are grown, starting with the wheat for the bread. Next, they'll study onions, mustard plants, tomatoes, lettuce and cucumbers. The exercise ends with a picture of a cow and calf, delicately teaching how we develop beef and cheese. This is a wonderful field trip for groups of at least 15 kids. Reservations are required.
Admission: $6 per person; Children under age 2 FREE
Time: M-F 9 am-2 pm
Physical location: 7705 FM 362 in Brookshire
www.DewberryFarm.com
866-908-FARM (866-908-276)

How would you rate this?

The month of May is dedicated to space exploration so drive south of Houston to the **Challenger Learning Center** at George Observatory, which is located in Brazos Bend State Park. Kids in first grade and up can explore space simulation or view solar flares through the telescopes. This is great for your young astronaut-to-be.
Recommended age: 6+ years
Admission: $5/person for all three telescopes and presentations
Time: Sat 3 pm-10 pm
Physical location: Brazos Bend State Park, one hour from downtown Houston

www.HMNS.org/See_Do/George_Observatory.asp

281-242-3055

How would you rate this? ☐ ☐

5/5: Do you know what Cinco de Mayo really stands for? According to MEXonline.com, "The holiday of Cinco De Mayo, The 5th Of May, commemorates the victory of the Mexican militia over the French army at The Battle Of Puebla in 1862... It is not, as many people think, Mexico's Independence Day, which is actually September 16."

This **Cinco de Mayo**, learn more about our neighbor Mexico by heading to the **Children's Museum of Houston**. Learn about the culture of Mexico by visiting the simulated Mexican village of **Yalálag**, where kids can barter for goods and learn Zapotec words as they explore the kid-sized town. Walk through the Zocalo to shop for food in the open-air market, take a ride on the VW bus, and see vivid photographs and authentic folk art from this town. Create pretend fireworks. Dance to maracas. Play a game of loteria, the Mexican bingo game.

Recommended age: 3+ years
Admission: $5
Time: 9 am–5 pm
Physical location: 1500 Binz in the Museum District
www.CMHouston.org 713-522-1138

How would you rate this? ☐ ☐

Load the kids in a wagon and head to **Everyones Art Car Parade** on Allen Parkway. Each spring, parade viewers see creativity at its finest with cars decorated in off-beat ways as well as a few classics. Kids of all ages enjoy the sights and sounds of this line up. Pack some sandwiches and drinks to enjoy during the procession. Arrive early for prime viewing. Parking is available along the parade route. Our family likes to grab a spot on Allen Parkway near the beginning of the parade route.

Recommended age: All

Admission: FREE

Time: Parade usually starts at 1 pm with the after-party "Traffic Jam" lasting until 5 pm. However, start times may change so check the Web site for updates.

Physical location: Allen Parkway at Taft and proceeding through downtown

www.OrangeShow.org 713-926-6368

How would you rate this?   ☐   ☐

Noah's Ark Pool is open May-September and is a creative way to swim. My daughter loved the water slides that are decorated with rainbows, animals and an ark, tying into the Biblical story. There are also several fountains that squirt water so the kids can dance in the water streams. There's also a larger pool for regular swimming. Lifeguards patrol all pools. As a parent, I like this pool park because it's small enough to allow parents to manage young swimmers, but still offers plenty to do. Gates open at 10 am. Tip: arrive early to avoid summer camps that typically visit around 1 pm.

Recommended age: All

Admission: $5 per person. Kids under age 2 are FREE.
Time: M-Sat 10 am–4 pm; Sun reserved for private parties only
Physical location: 10570 Westpark, Houston, TX 77042
www.FMHouston.com/Quillian/Quillian.aspx
832-668-1800

How would you rate this? ❑ ❑

Known as the "Home of the World's Largest Strawberry Shortcake," the **Strawberry Festival** offers food, arts and crafts, activities and entertainment for the whole family to enjoy in May. Buy a piece of the delicious strawberry shortcake and then leisurely walk the grounds. There's a variety of food to please everyone. Guests enjoy a petting zoo, pony rides, circus activities and traditional amusement park rides. If you live in central Houston, this is a good drive out so plan accordingly.

Recommended age: All
Admission: Adults $8; Children under 12: $4; Children under 5 FREE
Time: varies each year
Physical location: Pasadena Convention Center and Municipal Fairgrounds at 7902 Fairmont Parkway at Red Bluff Road in Pasadena.
www.StrawberryFest.org 281-991-9500

How would you rate this? ❑ ❑

Memorial Day is the last Monday in the month of May. This holiday is not just a good day off from work and school. Be sure to discuss the importance of Memorial Day with your family. Ask a veteran family member or friend to explain how he/she served in the military to ensure our freedoms today. Then head to the **Houston Heights World War II Memorial**. Planned, financed and constructed by Reagan High School alumni, this small memorial is a good visual reminder of the sacrifices others have made to maintain our freedom. There is also a grassy area where your family can have a picnic and enjoy the holiday.

Recommended age: All
Admission: FREE
Time: Dawn to dusk
Physical location: intersection of Heights Blvd. and 11th Street
www.HoustonHeightsOnline.com/WWWII Memorial.jpg

How would you rate this?

Memorial Day – Besides the regular exhibits available, the **Children's Museum of Houston** celebrates this holiday with kids. Children can make their own flag to take home and will hear a short presentation on the meaning of Memorial Day. Help your child make a Memorial Day flag to give to a veteran in your life.

Recommended age: 3+ years
Admission: $5; Kids under 2 are FREE

Time: 9 am–5 pm
Physical location: 1500 Binz in the Museum District
www.CMHouston.org 713-522-1138

How would you rate this?   ☐   ☐

Memorial Day – Enjoy a free day at the Houston Zoo. What a fun way to start your summer.
Recommended age: 1+ years
Admission: FREE
Time: 9 am-6 pm
Physical location: 1513 N. MacGregor
www.HoustonZoo.org 713-533-6500

How would you rate this?   ☐   ☐

The **FREE Family Film Festival** runs from June-August and allows youngsters to see select G and PG movies at no cost. Kids' meals are available for purchase. See the Web site for the schedule of movies.

Recommended age: 3+ years
Admission: FREE
Time: T-W at 10 am
Physical location: Edwards Houston Marq*e at 7620 Katy Freeway, Houston, TX 77024
www.RegMovies.com 713-263-7843

How would you rate this?

 Texans Youth Football Camps take place in June and July. Football players, ages 8-14, are instructed by top area high school coaches on the fundamentals of football in a program designed for beginners and experienced players. Athletes age 8-14 learn flag football while older kids try out tackle football. The camp includes daily visits and autographs from Texans players. All participants receive a camp jersey, four FREE training camp tickets and other great Texans giveaways. Plus, adult football fans will love hearing stories about the NFL players who guide their kids.

Recommended age: 8-14 years
Admission: ~$250
Time: most of the day
Physical location: Texans Practice Facility
www.HoustonTexans.com
E-mail **YouthFootball@HoustonTexans/com**

How would you rate this? ☐ ☐

The **AIA Sandcastle Competition** in Gal\
heats up each June. Have fun looking at the
wonders that folks create in the sand and gain
some inspiration for your own sandcastle. Bring a
backpack carrier for young kids and wear sandals
or flip flops that allow the sand to easily empty
from your shoes.
Recommended age: All
Admission: FREE but parking is $5 per entry.
Time: varies each year
Physical location: East Beach in Galveston
www.AIASandcastle.com 713-520-0155

How would you rate this? ☐ ☐

The **Houston Symphony** invites families
to participate in the Sounds Like Fun! series
throughout June and July. Entertain and educate
young audiences with the FREE concerts
throughout Houston neighborhoods. Enjoy an hour
performance with themes that delight children's
ears. Kids can feel free to dance along to the music.
Recommended age: 3+ years
Admission: FREE
Time: 10:30 am, 4 pm and 7:30 pm based on location
Physical location: 15 performances in greater Houston
**www.HoustonSymphony.org/Education/
Index.aspx**
713-238-1449 e&0@HoustonSymphony.com

How would you rate this? ☐ ☐

Ringling Bros. and Barnum & Bailey Circus
visits Houston each summer, usually in July. This is
true entertainment for all with morning, afternoon
and evening performances. The show lasts more than
two hours so it can be long for young children but
still eye-pleasing. Arrive an hour before the show to
see an elephant paint, try on a circus costume, meet
the clowns, shake paws with a performing pound
puppy and more. It's FREE with a paid ticket to the
show. After all, it's the greatest show on earth.
Recommended age: 3+ years
Admission: $12 per person and up
Time: various
Physical location: Reliant Stadium, 8334 Fannin
www.Ringling.com 832-667-1000

How would you rate this?

Buffalo Bayou Pontoon Boat Tours are an
exciting way to ride down Houston's bayou. Tours
to discover Houston's Mexican Free-tailed bat
colony run July-September on the second Friday
of the month. Tours last 1.5 hours and combine
fun with education. The pontoon boats are safe
and each passenger wears a personal flotation
device provided by your tour guide. Snacks are also
included – for the passengers, not the bats!
Recommended age: 7+ years
Admission: $15 per person
Time: F 7:30-9 pm
Physical location: Trips begin at 5000 Memorial Drive
www.BuffaloBayou.org 713-752-0314 x3 or
TSmith@BuffaloBayou.org

How would you rate this?

7/4: Independence Day – The **Children's Museum of Houston** features various activities to teach kiddos all about Independence Day. Create pretend fireworks with paper, glitter and glue. Discover the science between rockets, aerodynamics and chemical reactions. Starting at 9 am, kids can decorate a box as their special holiday parade float. Then, at 1 pm, children kick off the museum's July 4th parade and celebrate by marching with their floats throughout the museum.

Recommended age: 3+ years
Admission: $5; Kids under 2 are FREE
Time: 9 am–5 pm
Physical location: 1500 Binz in the Museum District
www.CMHouston.org 713-522-1138

How would you rate this? ☐ ☐

7/4: Independence Day – Celebrate American freedom by enjoying a free day at the **Houston Zoo**. This is an inexpensive way to spend the holiday as a family. Attend early to beat the heat.

Recommended age: 1+ years
Admission: FREE

Time: 9 am-6 pm
Physical location: 1513 N. MacGregor
www.HoustonZoo.org 713-533-6500

How would you rate this? ☐ ☐

7/4: Fireworks displays abound around town. Here are some fabulous ones. Before the fireworks shows, reassure your children and let kids know that the fireworks are loud but safe.

Check out an **Astros game**. Well, baseball IS the national pastime after all and our hometown heroes usually have a game over this holiday weekend. Who can turn down baseball and a hot dog over our Independence Day weekend? Besides the game, we love the fireworks display after evening games. Everyone just sits back in their chairs and RELAXES. The post-game traffic is a little lighter, too. This is a great way to spend the holiday.

Admission: Game tickets start at $7 each
Time: 1 pm, 3 pm, 6 pm or 7 pm, depending on the game schedule but fireworks follow evening games
Physical location: 501 Crawford Street in downtown Houston
www.Astros.com 713-259-8978

Galveston celebrates July 4th, starting with a parade through historic downtown Galveston. Next, a celebration is usually held including patriotic music and speeches, as well as refreshments. The fireworks begin around 9:15 pm and last about 25 minutes. The fireworks can be seen as far west as 81st and Seawall, and as far east as 14th and Seawall.
Recommended age: All
Admission: FREE

Time: 10 am-10 pm
Physical location: 37th Street and Seawall Blvd. in
Galveston
www.GalvestonCVB.com 888-425-4752

Pearland's Celebration of Freedom is an all-out family festival with craft booths and carnival rides. Admission is FREE but bring your wallet for all the food, music and rides.
Admission: FREE
Time: Noon-11 pm
Physical location: Independence Park, 3919 Liberty Dr., Pearland, TX 77581
www.ci.Pearland.tx.us

The **Freedom over Texas** celebration with fireworks takes place at Eleanor Tinsley Park along Buffalo Bayou. Children can enjoy plenty of activities throughout the day. In the evening, the whole family can share in the experience of listening to a live concert featuring several well-known performing artists and then watching the biggest fireworks display in greater Houston.
Admission: $6 per person; Kids 10 and under are FREE
Time: Noon-11 pm
Physical location: Eleanor Tinsley Park at Buffalo Bayou near downtown
www.HoustonTX.gov

Rosenberg's signature July 4th event
includes a concert, an inflatable carnival, KidZone,
horseshoes and washer tournaments, food and
refreshment vendors, hayrides through Seabourne
Creek Park, and a great fireworks show. Guests
are asked to bring their lawn chairs, their family
and all their friends, but to please leave the pets
and alcoholic refreshments at home.

General event parking is available immediately
south of the event site. Event parking and
handicapped parking can be found at the Rosenberg
Civic & Convention Center at 3825 Highway 36
South.
Admission: FREE
Time: 5-10 pm
*Physical location: Seabourne Creek Park located at
3831 Highway 36 South*
www.RosenbergTourism.com 832-595-3520

The **Annual Red, White and Bluefest** will be
held in Sugar Land at Oyster Creek and Lost Creek
parks. If you stay for the fireworks, it's a long
evening but a fun one. The holiday activities include
jugglers, magicians, a parade, music and fireworks.
Admission: FREE
Time: 4:30-11 pm
*Physical location: Oyster Creek and Lost Creek parks
but take the shuttle from Mercer Stadium at 16403
Lexington Blvd*
www.SugarlandTX.gov 281-275-2885

Houston Symphony's Star Spangled Salute:
Enjoy beautiful American tunes synchronized to the annual celebration at Miller Outdoor Theatre in Hermann Park in the museum district. Thousands flock to this event site and it remains a great family outing. Bring a large blanket to lie on the hill so your family can lean back, relaxing to the sights and sounds. Music plays until dark and is then accompanied by wonderful fireworks.
Admission: FREE
Time: 8:30-10:30 pm
Physical location: Hermann Park
www.HoustonSymphony.org

Annual Red, Hot and Blue Festival and Fireworks Extravaganza is a 23-minute fireworks show shot over The Woodlands Town Center. This is the second largest in the greater Houston region, second only to downtown Houston. The soundtrack for The Red, Hot & Blue Festival Fireworks is simulcast on Houston's Sunny 99.1 radio station.
Admission: FREE
Time: 6-10 pm
Physical location: 10001 Woodloch Forest Drive
www.Town-Center.com/RedHotBlue

Cool off in the pool at the **Fireworks Spectacular at Splashtown.** Catch a thrill speeding down a water slide. Kick summer into high gear. Celebrate America's Independence Day

with contests and entertainment for the entire family including fireworks at Six Flags' Splashtown.
Admission: $33 per person; Child under 48": $24.99; Kids 2 & Under: FREE
Time: 10 am-10 pm
Physical location: 21300 IH 45 N. in Spring
www.SixFlags.com/Parks/Splashtown
281-355-3300

Kemah Fireworks: If you have older kids, this is a fun outing. Stroll through the shops on the Kemah Boardwalk, enjoy a tasty dinner overlooking the water and then watch the fireworks show. This is the same show seen each Friday and Saturday throughout June and July. Remember to bring a change of clothes for kids who love to play in the dancing fountains.
Admission: FREE
Time: 9:30 pm
Physical location: Bradford and 2nd Street in Kemah
www.KemahBoardwalk.com
877-AT-KEMAH (887-285-3624)

How would you rate this?

 Take your child and his/her friend to the Film Festival at the **Wortham IMAX Theatre** at the Houston Museum of Natural Science. The festival runs from mid-August to September each year and offers about eight different films. Visit the Web site for a listing of this year's films and costs.

Recommended age: 5+ years
Admission: Adults $7; Children $5
Time: various from 10 am-8 pm
Physical location: One Hermann Circle Dr.
www.HMNS.org 713-639-4629

How would you rate this? ☐ ☐

September:

 Labor Day is the first Monday in September. Take a break from work and enjoy a free day at the Houston Zoo.
Recommended age: 1+ years
Admission: Free
Time: 9 am-6 pm
Physical location: 1513 N. MacGregor
www.HoustonZoo.org 713-533-6500

How would you rate this? ☐ ☐

9/24 is **Good Neighbor Day** and no matter where you live, you can always help a neighbor. Bake some cookies for your neighbors or color a picture for them. Take them a potted plant or fresh-cut flowers. Brainstorm the nice things you can do for neighbors and get started.
Recommended age: All
Admission: Free
Time: Any
Physical location: your neighborhood

The **Texas Renaissance Festival** runs on Saturdays and Sundays in October and November. As a fun family day, attendees can see 16th century costumes, cheer on jousting events, and enjoy festive food and music. Don't forget to see the glass blowing, make a candle of your own, and try your aim at archery. This is a full day.

Recommended age: 5+ years

Admission: Adults $21; Children $10. For discounts, purchase advance tickets. Games and rides are additional.

Time: 9 am-dusk

Physical location: From Houston, take I-45 north to Conroe. Exit Highway 105 west and turn left under the freeway. Follow Highway 105 approximately 20 miles to Plantersville. In Plantersville, turn left onto FM 1774 and go 6 miles to the festival entrance.

www.TexRenFest.com 800-458-3435

How would you rate this?

  Usually held in October, **Race for the Cure** in Houston is a moving experience for folks of all ages. Even if you're not a runner, sign up to walk the Kids K/Family Walk event and bring a stroller for younger children. Our family participated in Race for the Cure when our daughter was only seven months old. It's fantastic! Kids who are ready to give it their all are encouraged to participate with their parents/guardians in the noncompetitive 5K. All registrants receive a T-shirt and big congratulations. Youth participants receive either a bib or youth T-shirt. The Post-Race party is also tons of fun. What a great way to encourage children to contribute to the community by raising money to support a worthy cause.

Recommended age: 6 months+
Admission: $30/adult and $10/child
Time: 7:45-10 am
Physical location: Sam Houston Park in downtown
www.Komen-Houston.org

How would you rate this? ☐ ☐

Held in downtown Houston every October, the **Bayou City Art Festival** has been rated one of the top 200 events in the United States. Don't miss this annual event. (The festival is also held in Memorial Park in March.) Mingle with hundreds of artists from across the nation. Kids' activities include hat painting, sand blasting, jewelry making, hand wax sculptures and more. This is a rain or shine event.

Recommended age: 3+ years
Admission: Adults $8; Children under 12 FREE.
Time: 10 am–6 pm
Physical location: downtown Houston in front of City Hall and around Hermann Square on the streets of Walker, Bagby and McKinney.
www.BayouCityArtFestival.com 713-521-0133

How would you rate this? ☐ ☐

Enjoy safe Halloween trick-or-treating fun with a "naturally wild" twist at **Zoo Boo**'s "Main Events" during select October weekends. Zoo Boo features the kid-friendly "Happy Haunted House," an animal themed haunted house specially designed for little goblins 10 years of age and under with rooms created by seven local artists. Get in the spirit of Halloween with the Pumpkin Glow featuring 500 illuminated pumpkins each evening at the Zoo Reflection Pool, children's trick-or-treat and craft booths, costume parades and costume contests, special musical presentations, magic shows, and the stars of Zoo Boo – more that 3,100 animals from around the world. All Zoo Boo events are included in the regular price of admission.

Recommended age: 1+ years
Admission: Adults $8.50; Senior citizens $5; Children (age 2-11) $4; Children under 2 years free.
Time: 9 am-6 pm
Physical location: 1513 N. MacGregor
www.HoustonZoo.org 713-533-6500

How would you rate this?

The Houston Fire Museum sponsors **Fire Fest** each October to honor firefighters and educate Houstonians about what happens daily at fire stations throughout Houston. The Houston program is so well regarded that aspiring firefighters from all over come to Houston to train. This is a great way for your children to learn how the fire department serves Houstonians. Bring the kids to enjoy fire demonstrations, fire trucks, music, food and fun. Plus, children love to shake hands with real firefighters.

Recommended age: 3+ years
Admission: FREE
Time: 10 am–5 pm
Physical location: HFD Val Jahnke Training Facility at 8030 Braniff (off Telephone Rd. behind Hobby Airport)
www.HoustonFireMuseum.org 713-524-2526

How would you rate this?

Take your crew to a local pumpkin patch to jumpstart a festive mood in October. Our family favorite is **Dewberry Farm**. This attraction features the "Punkin Patch," where visitors take a short hayride to fields of pumpkins to make their selection. Kids enjoy the corn field maze, a barn full of farm animals, and a musical show. Little Farmersville is a play area for kids six and under, which includes tricycles, old fashioned rocking horses, hay stacks, and climbable tractor tires. Bring a hat to keep the sun and sand out of your eyes when it's dusty and windy. Wear closed-toe shoes and jeans for maximum comfort. Dewberry Farm just may become a new October tradition for your family, too. Call for directions or see the map online.

Recommended age: All ages
Admission: Children under age 2 free; Kids 2-12 $7; Adults $10; Senior citizens $8.50
Time: F 4-10 pm; Sat 10 am-9 pm; Sun noon-dusk
Physical location: 7705 FM 362 in Brookshire
www.DewberryFarm.com
866-908-FARM (866-908- 3276)

How would you rate this?

November:

With the Native Americans playing an important role in the tradition of Thanksgiving, consider how much your children know about this culturally rich group today. The **Alabama-Coushatta Indian Reservation** in Woodville (north of Houston) offers group tours of a real Indian reservation. A visit here is sure to spark conversations about the differences between how Native Americans live today and long ago. You'll spend a lot of time outdoors so dress warm and bring a coat. Avoid rainy days. This is a fun activity for classes or extracurricular activity groups.

Recommended age: 5+ years
Admission: $3/person
Time: 9 am-5 pm M-Sat; Closed Sun
Physical location: U.S 190 East, 571 State Park Road 56 in Livingston
www.Alabama-Coushatta.com 936-563-1329

How would you rate this?

11/12 is **Veterans Day**. Don't forget to thank a veteran for fighting for American freedoms.

November-January, Moody Gardens features the **Festival of Lights**. Bring the entire family to view acres of lights and holiday music. Grab a pair of ice skates and glide across the outdoor ice rink, too. Santa Claus often visits the festival, so be good! Moody Gardens is open Christmas Eve and Christmas Day.

Recommended age: All ages

Admission: $6 per person with FREE admission for children under 3. For an additional $4 per person, visitors can also take advantage of the holiday IMAX movies, participate in the holiday movie ride, walk through the rainforest, etc.

Time: 6-9 pm

Physical location: 1 Hope Blvd. in Galveston

www.MoodyGardens.com 800-582-4673

How would you rate this?

 The evening of Thanksgiving, the City of Houston kicks off the holiday season in grand style with the **Lighting of S. Post Oak Boulevard** in the Galleria area. Fun for the entire family, Houston lights its outdoor Christmas trees and decorations to turn bustling blocks into glistening gems. Typical features include performances by local choruses, brief reenactments from the Houston Ballet's Nutcracker, and a fireworks display to conclude the evening. Parents can purchase hot cocoa and cider from some of the nearby hotels. Children love the holiday souvenirs that vendors sell on the street. And, of course, Santa makes an appearance as well. This is an all-time family favorite.

Recommended age: All ages

Admission: FREE

Time: Dusk
Physical location: S. Post Oak Boulevard (between San
Felipe and Westheimer)
www.HoustonTx.gov

How would you rate this? ☐ ☐

Each year on the Friday following Thanksgiving, families can enjoy a free day at the **Houston Zoo**. Plus, it's a great way to walk off all the turkey and treats.
Recommended age: 1+ years
Admission: FREE
Time: 9 am-6 pm
Physical location: 1513 N. MacGregor
www.HoustonZoo.org 713-533-6500

How would you rate this? ☐ ☐

Late November through December: **Houston Ballet** presents **The Nutcracker** each holiday season and it's another wonderful way to kick off the holidays. Children love the flying bakers, dancing sweets and snow-filled scenes. Adults can explain the story before the performance begins so youngsters understand the unfolding tale. Arrive early to be seated.
Recommended age: 5+ years
Admission: Tickets begin at $22
Time: 2 pm and 7:30 pm performances
Physical location: Brown Theater at Wortham Theater
Center at 501 Texas Avenue near Smith St.
www.HoustonBallet.org 713-523-6300

How would you rate this? ☐ ☐

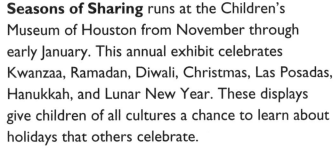

Seasons of Sharing runs at the Children's Museum of Houston from November through early January. This annual exhibit celebrates Kwanzaa, Ramadan, Diwali, Christmas, Las Posadas, Hanukkah, and Lunar New Year. These displays give children of all cultures a chance to learn about holidays that others celebrate.

Recommended age: 3+ years
Admission: $5; Th 5-8 pm are free; $3 T – Sun 3-5 pm
Time: T-Sat 9 am-5 pm; Sun noon-5 pm
Physical location: 1500 Binz in the Museum District
www.CMHouston.org 713-522-1138

How would you rate this?

December:

December marks the beginning of **Holiday Lights in Hermann Park**, Houston's version of "Central Park." The event usually begins at 6 pm with the lighting at the Jones Reflection Pool. Children of all ages enjoy the holiday production presented by the Hermann Park Conservancy. Then, Houston families enjoy the lights on weekends throughout the month 6-9 pm. Pack up the kids with bikes, trikes or even roller blades and put that energy to good use. This makes a nice alternative to the usual after-dinner routine. Strollers are welcome.

Recommended age: All
Admission: FREE
Time: 6-9 pm
Physical location: 6001 Fannin between the Museum District, Texas Medical Center, Rice University and

Highway 288. The closest Metro Rail stop is Hermann Park/Rice University.
www.HermanPark.org 713-524-5876

How would you rate this? ❑ ❑

A part of Texas' internationally renowned Victorian Christmas Festival, **Dickens on the Strand** in Galveston recreates the era of Charles Dickens and is a traditional holiday activity on the first weekend of December each year. Families can walk the 10-block area in Galveston to see how characters from Dickens' stories lived. Costumed vendors and performers stroll about to entertain all. Children's activities include visiting the Royal Menagerie Petting Zoo, taking a ride on a pony or elephant, playing in the "Snow on Sunday," joining in the Scrooge's Scavenger Hunt, hearing a storyteller, participating in a Backyard Circus, joining in the Puppet Parade or doing crafts and other projects. Strollers are welcome.
Recommended age: All
Admission: Adult tickets are $10 in advance and $12 at the gate. Children age 7 -12 are $4 in advance and $6 at the gate. Children under 6 are FREE. Attendees dressed in full Victorian costume are admitted FREE.
Time: Sat 10 am-9 pm and Sun 10 am-6 pm
Physical location: the Strand National Historic Landmark District in Galveston
www.DickensOnTheStrand.org 409-765-7834

How would you rate this? ❑ ❑

The **Houston Symphony's annual Christmas Family Concert** falls on the second Saturday in December. "How the Grinch Stole Christmas" is an example of a previous production. The symphony offers a charming way to spend a morning as a family during the holidays. Youngsters can participate in arts and crafts before and after the children's show. Each performance usually includes singing, dancing, costumes and a visit from Santa.

Recommended age: 4+ years
Admission: Adults $15; Children $9
Time: 10 am and 11:30 am performances
Physical location: courtyard level of Jones Hall at 615 Louisiana St. in downtown
www.HoustonSymphony.org/Education
713-224-7575

How would you rate this?

There's just nothing like packing the car full of kids, blankets and hot cocoa to drive around town looking at **holiday lights**. Local TV news stations usually highlight some extra bright neighborhoods. Two favorite neighborhoods are **Shepherd Park Plaza** and **Candlelight Plaza** that have holiday-themed streets. The **Heights** also has festive lights. Sing carols and don't forget the candy canes.

Recommended age: All ages
Admission: FREE
Time: After dusk
Physical location: Neighborhoods throughout Houston
How would you rate this?

Count your blessings. No matter what your race or religion, all of us can recognize how blessed we are. This holiday season, **give back to your community** by encouraging children to participate in the giving (not just receiving). Children can do extra chores to earn money to donate to the Salvation Army collection spots around town. Load up some nonperishable goods and take them to the Houston Food Bank so that others have plenty of food this season. Do a good deed just to help another and reap the reward of knowing you made someone else feel special.

Recommended age: 1+ years

Admission: FREE

Time: various

Physical location: various donation locations throughout Houston

www.SalvationArmyHouston.org

713-752-0677

www.HoustonFoodBank.org 713-223-3700

www.khou.com/Community

How would you rate this?

A candlelight Christmas is available at **Washington on the Brazos** State Historical Site in Washington (about an hour drive northwest of Houston). Hear stories of Christmas customs and traditions celebrated in 19th century Texas. Enjoy music, carols, buggy rides, and arts and crafts to take home. You can even decorate the historic house for the holiday.

Recommended age: 1+ year

Admission: Adults $6; Children $4

Time: varies each year
Physical location: 12300 Park Road 12 in Washington, Texas
www.BirthPlaceOfTexas.com 936-878-2213

How would you rate this?

New Year's Noon Celebration at the Children's Museum features lots of fun for youngsters. Museum employees guide children in hat making, float construction and other fun activities from 9:30–11:30 am. The kids' celebratory parade begins at 11:45 am and culminates with the sparkling ball drop at noon. Kids can then enjoy dance fever until 12:30 pm, followed by crazy hat making and other arts and crafts until 3 pm. This event is a great way for your little ones to partake in the New Year's festivities.

Recommended age: 3+ years
Admission: $5 per person
Time: 9 am-6 pm
Physical location: 1500 Binz in the Museum District
www.CMHouston.org 713-522-1138

How would you rate this?

There is a **New Year's Eve Skate Party** at the Dairy Ashford Roller Rink for children. Don't worry: you can pick your kids up before the ball drops so they have an enjoyable evening and are still in bed at a decent hour.

Recommended age: age 8+ years
Admission: $20 per person includes skate rental and skating, hats, horns, balloons, food ticket for a small

drink and the choice of one hot dog or a slice of pizza.
Time: 6 pm-2 am
Physical location: 1820 Dairy Ashford
www.SkateDARR.com 281-493-5651

How would you rate this? ☐ ☐

Get to know the roots of Houston by visiting **Allen's Landing**. This park on Buffalo Bayou marks the spot where the Allen brothers began the new town called Houston in 1836. Walk through some restored 19th-century buildings. Enjoy the small park amid the skyscrapers. Head out early to avoid the heat and then check out one of the great restaurants in downtown Houston.

Recommended age: All

Admission: FREE

Time: Dawn to dusk

Physical location: 1001 Commerce Street; bordered by Travis, Milam, Congress, and Preston St.

www.BuffaloBayou.org/AllensLanding.html

How would you rate this?

The **Alley Theatre** features a wonderful program called **Family Day Out** throughout the year as a chance for parents to see an Alley performance while their 6-10 year old children participate in a creative drama workshop. Parents attend adult plays while their children attend creative drama workshops to learn about play productions.

Recommended age: Adults for theatre but children 6-10 years for the drama workshop

Admission: $10 per child with the purchase of a theatre ticket

Time: Children must be checked in by 2 pm and performances begin at 2:30 pm.

Physical location: 615 Texas Avenue in downtown Houston

www.AlleyTheatre.org
Tickets: 713-228-8421;
Questions: 713-228-9341 ext. 425

How would you rate this?

Visit Houston's **outdoor sanctuaries** to see
nature flourishing in the midst of a bustling city.
Take a walk through the woods and talk to your
children about the different plants and animals
living here. Even children too young to walk can
enjoy the view if an adult brings a backpack harness
to carry them in. Older children can discuss
where animals might live and what makes those
places safe. This is a good way to encourage an
appreciation for nature and comfort in it. Visit
in the spring or fall to escape harsher weather
elements.
Recommended age: All ages
Admission: Exploring on your own is FREE. Classes
range in price from $12-$15.

Arboretum
Time: Dawn to dusk
Physical location: 4501 Woodway Dr. within
Memorial Park
www.HoustonArboretum.org/ 713-681-8433
Note: Enjoy the five-mile track and numerous
interactive exhibits in the Nature Center. Various
classes are also available for kids age 3-5 and 5-12.

Edith L. Moore Nature Sanctuary
Time: Dawn to dusk
Physical location: 440 Wilchester off Memorial
www.HoustonArboretum.org/ 713-932-1639

Note: This location has 18 acres to explore and is an excellent birding site. No camping or picnics are allowed.

Jesse H. Jones Park & Nature Center
Time: Dawn to dusk
Physical location: 20634 Kenswick Drive in Humble
www.HCP4.net/Jones
Note: This park includes 225 acres of land and has a paved handicap-friendly trail. Picnic areas are also available.

Mercer Arboretum and Botanic Gardens
Time: M-Sat 8 am–7 pm; Sun 10 am–7 pm
Physical location: 22306 Aldine Westfield
www.cp4.hctx.net/Mercer 281-443-8731
Note: This is a 214 acre park with picnic areas.

How would you rate this?

 Barnes & Noble Story Time is a great way to encourage your children to read while making neighborhood friends. Several Houston-area stores offer weekly story time for young kids.
Recommended age: 3+ years
Admission: FREE
Physical locations and times:

Vanderbilt Square
3003 W Holcombe Blvd
Houston, TX 77025
713-349-0050
T 10:30-11:30 am elementary students;
W 10:30-11:30 am preschool students

Town & Country Center
12850 Memorial Drive Suite 1600
Houston, TX 77024
713-465-5616
Th 11 am-noon ages 3-6 years

Copperfield
7026 Hwy 6 North
Houston, TX 77095
281-861-6842
Th 10:30-11:30 am ages 3-6 years

Humble
20131 Highway 59
Humble, TX 77338
281-540-3060
W 11 am-noon ages 3-6 years

The Woodlands Mall
1201 Lake Woodlands Dr. #3008
The Woodlands, TX 77381
281-465-8744
M 11 am-noon ages 3-6 years

www.BarnesAndNoble.com

How would you rate this? ☐ ☐

The **Bayou Wildlife Park** in Alvin is a miniature safari for families to explore without traveling across time zones. Take a ride on the Exotic Tram to see the wildlife. Kids like the pony rides and petting zoo. Avoid rainy days as this park is less enjoyable when the grounds are soggy.

Recommended age: 1+ year

Admission: Adults $9; Children $5.50

Time: March-August: 10 am-4pm; August-February: 10 am-3:30 pm; Closed M

Physical location: 5050 FM 517 RD in Alvin

www.bayouwildlifepark.com 281-337-6376

How would you rate this?

What's the most popular flavor of ice cream? Find out at the **Blue Bell Creamery** in Brenham, Texas. Okay, so it's outside Houston, but it's too tasty to miss. Hungry? Tours last 45 minutes and are scheduled throughout the day. See the steps taken to make this frozen dessert and how they add the real fruit. You'll even see where they make popsicles and ice cream sandwiches. Each tour ends at the country store with a tasty treat of ice cream included in admission. Yummy! Kids also receive old-fashioned paper hats. Yes, employees may eat all the ice cream they want while on duty and receive discounts on take-home ice cream. The yard in front of the creamery provides a cute photo op. Call ahead because I've found Blue Bell is often closed on special days.

Recommended age: 3+ years

Admission: Adults $3; Senior Citizens and Kids 6-14 $2; Kids under 6 FREE.

Time: Tours are scheduled M–F 10 am, 11 am, 1 pm, 1:30 pm and 2 pm but families can visit the creamery for a taste test on Sat.

Physical location: 1101 South Horton in Brenham, TX.
From Houston, take Hwy. 290 to Brenham. Turn right
on FM 577 and continue 2 miles.
www.BlueBell.com 979-836-7977
How would you rate this?   ☐   ☐

Head indoors for some fun at a **Build-A-Bear Workshop**®. Children can design their own bear or other critter and learn the process of making stuffed animals. Participants stuff the fuzzy animals, make hearts for the loved ones, print birth certificates, and select a miniature house (a take-home box) for the newborn animal.
Recommended age: 5+ years
Admission: $10-$25 for a bear or critter + optional
accessories; under $40 total
Time: M-Sat 10 am-9 pm; Sun 11 am-7 pm
Physical location: Galleria Mall at 5085 Westheimer
Road, #3605; 713-355-3388
Memorial City Mall located near Gessner and I-10;
713-468-6987
www.BuildABear.com

How would you rate this?   ☐   ☐

Another inexpensive activity in Memorial City Mall is riding the **Carousel**. Located on the south side of the mall near the food court, the two-level carousel is quite a fantasy. After a short trip around, grab a bite to eat from one of the many restaurants nearby.
Recommended age: 36" tall minimum to ride without
a guardian; Children under 36" tall may ride with an

accompanying guardian, who rides for FREE.
Admission: $1
Time: M-Sat 10 am-9 pm; Sun noon-6 pm
Physical location: Memorial City Mall at I-10 and
Gessner

www.MemorialCityMall.com 713-464-8640

How would you rate this?

Spring has sprung at **The Cockrell Butterfly Center** at the Houston Museum of Natural Science. See beautifully colored butterflies from around the globe and watch baby butterflies hatch from cocoons. Walk through the indoor rain forest to enjoy butterflies flying about, see fish in cavernous aquariums and iguanas lurking in the bushes. Visit the Insect Zoo to see beetles, hissing cockroaches, and more. Kids must be old enough to walk on their own because strollers are not allowed.

Recommended age: 3+ years
Admission: Adults $6; Children $4. Kids under age 3 are FREE.
Time: 9 am-9 pm
Physical location: One Hermann Circle Drive
www.HMNS.org 713-639-4629

How would you rate this?

Each Friday and Saturday morning at 11:45, the Angelika Film Center presents **The Cry Baby Matinee** for parents all over Houston. Relax and enjoy a film at the Angelika without worrying about breastfeeding in the dark or squelching unexpected hissyfits. The theater dims the lights (rather than turns them off), lowers the volume, and rolls the film. The theater even provides changing tables at the front of the auditorium for diaper changing during the shows. This is a perfect outing when the weather outside is less than ideal, but appreciated year-round. An added bonus: the theater is not packed with movie goers so you and your little one have plenty of space.

Recommended age: adults with children under 5 years
Admission: Adults $6; Children under 5 FREE.
Time: 11:45 am
Physical location: 510 Texas Avenue (at the corner of Smith)
www.AngelikaFilmCenter.com/Houston
713-CALL-AFC (713-225-5232)

How would you rate this?

Be sure to visit the **Downtown Aquarium** for a true delight. The numerous aquarium exhibits amaze children of all ages. For a short visit, head to the Downtown Aquarium restaurant where visitors can view stingrays, eels and more while eating a meal. A kids' menu with coloring activities is an added bonus.

If your group has an afternoon or more, enjoy all that this attraction offers. Besides the amazing aquarium itself, kids can also enjoy an educational train ride around the park, various amusement park rides (including the 100-foot ferris wheel), and games. Tip: bring a change of clothes or swim suit

so your little ones can play in the dancing fou
at the entrance to the rides and enjoy the mi
on a hot day.

Recommended Age: 3+ years
Admission: Pay $16 to take advantage of the aquarium
and all rides, instead of paying individual ticket prices.
Time: Sun-Th 10 am-10 pm; F-Sat 10 am-11 pm
Physical location: 410 Bagby St. and Memorial Dr. in
downtown Houston
www.DowntownAquariumHouston.com
or call 713-223-FISH(3474).

How would you rate this?

My favorite soft drink is Diet Dr Pepper so I
couldn't resist a tour of the **Dr Pepper Bottling
Company**. You can see how that drink gets into
all those cans and bottles. Watch a video about
the history of Dr Pepper. And yes, you'll get to
do a taste test, too. Tours are conducted only on
Thursdays at 9 am and children must be at least six
years old. Reservations are required but this is a
great field trip.

Recommended age: 6+ years
Admission: FREE
Time: Th 9 am
Physical location: 2400 Holly Hall
www.DrPepper.com 713-799-1024 x7193 for
information and reservations

How would you rate this?

A trip to **Farmers Market** is a treat any time of year, but visits during cooler months are most enjoyable since there is no air conditioning. (There are some indoor/outdoor fans though.) Not only can adults get good deals on fresh fruit and vegetables from area farmers, but they can also use this as an opportunity to teach children how food arrives at the store by speaking with the local merchants. Plants and flowers are also available as well as seasonal items such as piñatas, pumpkins, etc. This is a stroller-friendly place. Avoid pushing a stroller and a shopping cart by bringing a large mesh bag to carry purchases. Wear cool, comfortable clothes. No checks accepted.

Recommended age: All ages
Admission: No cost to enter. Goods are marked for retail, but some vendors will barter.
Time: 6 am-8:30 pm daily
Physical location: 2520 Airline near I-45 North
713-862-4027

How would you rate this?

Drive down to **Galveston** for some fun in the sun. Pack a lunch, drinks, beach towels and sand toys for a day of entertainment. Don't forget your sun block. Beaches to try are: Galveston Island State Park, Stewart Beach (includes a playground) and the pocket beaches on the west end of the island. Another option is to visit Moody Gardens' beach with imported white sand. (See Moody Gardens entry in No Reason for a Season section.) The beach on the seawall across from the San Luis Resort is regularly groomed.

Recommended age: 1 + years
Admission: Fees begin at $3 depending upon which beach you visit.
Time: Dawn to dusk
Physical location: various

www.Galveston.com
888-GAL-ISLE (888-425-4753)

How would you rate this?

Enjoy a ferry ride by driving or walking about the **Galveston Island Ferry**. The ride covers 2.7 miles to Port Bolivar with views of the Bolivar Lighthouse and Seawolf Park. The ferry runs 24 hours a day and is a fun, free ride. Avoid the crowds by attending during the week in the summer or weekends of non-summer months.
Recommended age: All ages
Admission: FREE
Time: 24 hours
Physical location: End of Ferry Road in Galveston
409-763-2386

How would you rate this?

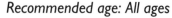

Visit the Heights during the **Heights First Saturday** celebration to see local talent and enjoy a small town feeling within this big city. Browse various forms of art and jewelry and purchase a favorite. Stroll the streets to see unique stores in a friendly atmosphere. The Yale Street Arts Market is part of the Heights First Saturday event and includes many artists who create items just for children such as clothes, toys and decorations. Free trolley tours are available from 12:30 pm–4 pm. This event is held the first Saturday of each month. Some Saturdays also include plays and puppet shows for children. What a fun way to get familiar with the historic Houston Heights.

Recommended age: All

Admission: FREE

Time: 9 am–5 pm but most people head there around 11 am

Physical location: Trolley tour begins at Hickory Hollow Restaurant at 101 Heights Boulevard. The Yale Street Arts Market is located at 210 West 21st Street – ½ a block off Yale.

www.HeightsFurstSaturday.com 713-802-1213
www.YaleStreetMarket.com

How would you rate this?

The **Houston Ballet** performs numerous productions throughout the year for varying age groups. Performances range from Madame Butterfly to modern dances to popular rock tunes. Arrive early to be seated because once the show begins, you will struggle to find your seat in the dimmed theater.

Recommended age: 5+ years, depending on the ballet

Admission: Tickets begin at $17

Time: 2 pm and 7:30 pm productions

Physical location: Brown Theater at Wortham Theater Center at 501 Texas Avenue near Smith St.

www.HoustonBallet.org 713-523-6300

How would you rate this?

Children love the **Houston Museum of Natural Science** for its wonderful exhibits. The dinosaurs are always a big hit, but don't miss the other exhibits focusing on Texas wildlife, gems and minerals, and much more. Adults can walk kids through the exhibits and explain what each describes. Children can then discuss their thoughts and reactions. The Fondren Discovery Place is an interactive, permanent exhibit for kids, so check that out, too.

Recommended age: 3+ years
Admission: Adults $7; Children $4.
Time: 9 am-9 pm
Physical location: One Hermann Circle Drive
www.HMNS.org 713-639-4629

How would you rate this?

Want to teach your little ones about the importance of police officers? Visit the **Houston Police Museum**, where they can see various guns, knives and other weapons that officers use to protect Houstonians. Old and new uniforms are also on view. Encourage your children to talk to the police officers at the museum so kids learn to trust these authority figures. Guided tours are available some days, but tours on your own allow you to go at the right pace for your family. Try to park in the circular drive for ease.

Recommended age: 3+ years
Admission: FREE
Time: M-F 8 am–4 pm
Physical location: 17000 Aldine Westfield Rd. near

Intercontinental Airport
www.HoustonTx.gov/Police/History.htm
281-230-2360

How would you rate this? ☐ ☐

The **Houston Symphony** presents its Explorer Concert (formerly called Discoverer concert) which combines music and academic curriculum. Productions differ each year but continually remain an ideal field trip. Hands-on activities are available in the lobby before the first show and following the second performance.
Recommended age: 8+ years
Admission: $4 per student with one free adult permitted for every 10 students
Time: usually 11:15 am performance
Physical location: courtyard level of Jones Hall at 615 Louisiana St. in downtown
www.HoustonSymphony.org/Education
713-224-7575

How would you rate this? ☐ ☐

Discover the underground world of downtown Houston with the **Houston Tunnel System**. The tunnel covers 7 miles of walkways with air conditioning, restaurants, shops and more. Take the kids to explore this feature and grab a bite to eat at a local eatery. Free parking is available near Milam and Prairie. Don't forget to stop by the colorful sculpture on Milam at the JP Morgan Chase Bank Building. My daughter loved it.

Recommended age: All ages.
Admission: The tunnel is FREE but guided tours are available for $20 per adult and $10 per child.
Time: Weekdays 7 am–6 pm; Sat 10 am–3 pm
Physical location: Twenty feet below downtown Houston. Try starting at Texas St. and Prairie St.
www.HoustonDowntown.com
www.DiscoverHoustonTexas.com
713-222-WALK (9255)

How would you rate this?

 Beat the heat by **ice skating**. This is a lot of fun and it's not often that Houstonians see ice. Classes and summer camps are also available for the cautious. Ready for a break? Watch the competitive skaters twirl on the ice. The ice rinks are open daily but hours vary.
Recommended age: 5+ years
Polar Ice Galleria
Recommended age: 5+ years
Admission: Children under 12 $6.50, plus skate rental of $3
Time: M-Th 11 am-5 pm and 8-10 pm; F 11 am-10 pm; Sat 12:30-10 pm; Sun 1-9 pm
Physical location: within the Houston Galleria mall at 610 and Westheimer
www.PolarIceGalleria.com 713-621-1500

How would you rate this?

Ice Skate USA
Admission: Adult $6.50 + $3 skate rental; Children under 10 and seniors $5.50 + $3 skate rental; Children

5 and under $3.50 (including skate rental)
Time: M and W 10-Noon and 12:15-3:15; T and Th
10-noon, 12:15-3:15 and 3:30-5 pm; F 10 am-6 pm
and 8-10 pm; Sat-Sun 1:30-4 pm
Physical location: within Memorial City Mall located at
I-10 and Gessner
www.ShopMemorialCity.com/Dining Events/
Ice Skate.html 713-463-9296

How would you rate this? ☐ ☐

Climb Mount Everest and fly through Grand
Canyon all in one sitting. The Wortham **IMAX
Theatre** is a cinematic experience for kids young
and old. Parents won't mind sitting through these
movies. And you won't mind visiting it again and
again. Visitors learn about various continents
without needing a passport, and the travels are fun.
Recommended age: 5+ years
Admission: Adults $7; Children $5.
Time: 9 am-9 pm with shows throughout the day
Physical location: in Houston Museum of Natural
Science at One Hermann Circle Dr.
www.hmns.org 713-639-4629

How would you rate this? ☐ ☐

Jumpin Jak's Party Place is an indoor
playground with something for almost everyone.
There's even a seating area for parents to watch
the kids go wild. The great thing is that your family
will stay cool while climbing wood structures and
crawling through mazes. For younger kids, a pit of

balls is available that is only knee deep for toddlers and is safe. Parents can climb in, too.

Recommended age: 1+ years
Admission: ages 1-3 pay your age; ages 4-12: $4
Time: M-F 9 am-9 pm (weekends for birthday parties only)
Physical location: 3403 FM 1960 between Veterans Memorial & Kuykendahl
www.JumpinJaks.net 281-537-8833

How would you rate this? ☐ ☐

Much like the Downtown Aquarium (since they're owned and operated by the same company), the **Kemah Boardwalk** is great, especially for toddlers and young kids. In addition to the amazing aquarium and restaurant like the Houston version, the Kemah Boardwalk has more restaurants, shops and rides. For example, your family can take a 20-minute ride on Galveston Bay aboard the Boardwalk BEAST boat. (Adults $12 and children $9). Tackle the rock wall and enjoy the rides and scenery.

The good news? Kids one year and younger ride the kiddie rides (carousel, train, etc.) for FREE. During our short trip, we paid $20 for a two-person lunch but got FREE parking, boat shuttle, carousel ride and run through the fountains. If you plan to stay longer, an all-day ride pass for $16 is a good bet. There was still plenty more to do. Bring a change of clothes and a towel because kids love to play in the dancing fountains and they'll get wet aboard the BEAST. Kemah Boardwalk is a good option for folks living east of the 610 loop (Pearland, Friendswood, etc.) Otherwise, the Downtown Aquarium is a shorter drive with a few less attractions.

Recommended Age: 1+ years
Admission: FREE to stroll the area but lunch, aquarium and rides are additional
Time: Sun–Th 11 am–10 pm; F–Sat 11 am–11 pm
Physical location: Bradford and 2nd Street, Kemah, TX. 77565
www.KemahBoardwalk.com 281-334-7575

How would you rate this?

Our family loved the **King's Orchard** in Plantersville. Bring your kids to this real orchard to pick fresh fruit, vegetables and beautiful flowers. At only a year old, my daughter had a ball picking blackberries and flowers for mommy. Remember that this is at least an hour's drive from Houston so pack books or entertainment for the car ride. Plan on spending the better part of a day here. Tips: wear closed-toe shoes and sun block. Bring water bottles because it gets hot out there. Arrive early to beat the heat.

Recommended age: 1+ year
Admission: Pay for the items you pick.
Time: T-F 8am-5pm; Sat-Sun 7am-5pm; Closed M
Physical location: 11282 County Road 302 in Plantersville
www.KingsOrchard.com 936-894-2766

How would you rate this?

Laser Quest Houston is a fun indoor activity that keeps everyone on the move. Players use harmless laser guns and equipment to tag opponents. Crawl around hideouts and structures to avoid being hit. Split your family up into teams and engage in a friendly competition. Afterward, grab a drink to refresh.

Recommended age: 8+ years
Admission: $7.50 per person per game
Time: Westheimer location is open M-Th 5-9 pm; F 4-11 pm; Sat noon-11 pm; Sun noon-7 pm
Champions location has the same hours except it's open until 8 pm Sun.
Physical locations:
13711 Westheimer Road Unit H, Houston 77707; 281-596-9999
Champions Village Shopping Center 6560 FM 1960 West, Houston 77069; 281-397-6612
www.LaserQuest.com

How would you rate this?

 A young artist in bloom? **The Mad Potter** offers children (and adults) a chance to get creative by painting and customizing items such as dinner plates, ice cream bowls, banks (various shapes), figurines and more. Spend a few minutes choosing an item to decorate and then take an hour or two painting your work. The store will glaze and fire these creations for pick up later in the week. These also make great holiday gifts.

Recommended age: 5+ years
Admission: $8 per child painter + $8-$16 per pottery piece

Time: All stores are open daily but hours of operation vary.

Physical locations: The Mad Potter River Oaks at 1963-A West Gray; 713-807-8900

The Mad Potter West at 1341 S. Voss Rd.; 713-278-7300

The Mad Potter Bellaire at 4882 Beechnut at 610; 713-664-8808

The Mad Potter Sugar Land at 4787 Sweetwater at Highway 59; 281-313-0555

www.TheMadPotter.com

How would you rate this?

Return to the downtown streets and head to Main Street, where the **Metro Rail** runs. The Metro Rail has gotten some flack for safety but we loved our ride. The rail is clearly marked and safe. I bought two all-day passes for $2.50 from the ticket machines at the Metro stop. I didn't even need to buy that much but as a first-timer, I wasn't sure. We met lots of Houstonians riding the Metro Rail and enjoyed our tour of downtown Houston. We decided to end our stop at Hermann Park but since it was pouring down rain, we headed back north on the Metro Rail for our second ride. From end to end, a one-way ride will last 32 minutes. It was easy and inexpensive fun for my daughter. I highly recommend it. Tips: wear shorts and walking shoes. Use a backpack so you can best help your child cross the busy streets while holding his/her hand.

Recommended age: All

Admission: $2/person for all-day pass with unlimited rides
Time: Weekdays 4:30 am-2:30 am; Sat 5:30 am-2:15 am; Sun 10 pm-12:45 am
Physical location: Main Street downtown
www.RideMetro.org 713-635-4000

How would you rate this?

 The **Milky Way Play Castle** is a big hit with kids at Memorial City Mall on the west side of Houston. This is a good way to beat the Houston heat or have fun on a rainy day. This colorful playground measures 21 feet high and includes a slide, bridge, crawling tunnels, a pretend moat and mushroom-like stepping stones. Seats around the perimeter are available for adults. Conveniently park your stroller within the castle grounds. The play castle is open daily during mall hours and allows young children to kick off their shoes and roam freely.
Recommended age: 48" tall maximum; 1+ year
Admission: FREE
Time: M-Sat 10 am-9 pm; Sun noon-6 pm
Physical location: Memorial City Mall at I-10 and Gessner
www.memorialcitymall.com 713-464-8640

How would you rate this?

 Moody Gardens in Galveston offers wonderful options, no matter what the weather. Kids will enjoy the aquarium, where they may touch a live starfish and cheer on the performing seals. Or travel through Moody Garden's rainforest, where children can spy exotic birds flying from tree to tree as they chirp merrily. Many kids will also enjoy the bat cave, where they learn how bats hang upside down. If that's not enough, there's also the Discovery Pyramid, where guides share educational details on space craft. Children under 3 are admitted free, but there's not much they can engage in. This is also a good place to host a birthday party.

Recommended age: 3+ years
Admission: A day pass for $35 may be the best option to take advantage of it all.
Time: 10 am-8 pm during summer; 10 am-6 pm during school year
Physical location: One Hope Boulevard in Galveston
www.MoodyGardens.org 800-582-4673

How would you rate this?

 While at college at SMU in Dallas, I loved the fresh smell of **Mrs. Baird's Bakery** that filled the air for over a mile. I should have known about the Houston tours. Take your youngsters on a tour of this bakery for an interesting field trip or a fun activity on your own. You'll learn how Mrs. Baird makes all that wonderful bread and breakfast treats. Tip: During warm months, schedule your tour in the morning to avoid the extreme heat or visit during the winter for a great warm up.

Children must be at least six to take this tour and one adult is required for every 10 kids. For

safety reasons, no open-toed shoes are all
Reservations at least two weeks in advan
required.
Recommended age: 6+ years
Admission: FREE
Time: Tours are available Th 10 am–2 pm
Physical location: 6650 N. Houston Rosslyn Rd.
http://MrsBairds.com/Fun/Visit.html

How would you rate this?

 Sundays Are Family Days at the **Museum of Fine Arts Houston** (MFAH) but other days are fun for the artist in your family. Kids and adults enjoy learning about art through Creation Station, a drop-in studio workshop. Families make their own paintings, sculpture, prints, photographs and more. Storytelling in the Galleries links art and literature for children, and provides an opportunity for children to create art after hearing stories.
Recommended age: 5+ years
Admission: Children $3.50; Adults $7; Children age 6-18 who show a Houston Public Library Power Card, Harris County Public Library Card, or any other Public Library Card are admitted FREE on Sat and Sun. Th are FREE for all.
Time: Closed M; T-W 10 am-5 pm; Th 10 am-9 pm; F-Sat 10 am-7 pm; Sun 12:15-7 pm
Physical location: 1001 Bissonnet Street
www.MFAH.org 713-639-7300

How would you rate this?

Hana & Arthur Ginzbarg **Nature Discovery Center** is an amazing way to explore nature and its critters. The second floor of a house has been dedicated as the Discovery Room, featuring lots of hands-on learning experiences for children. One room has a wonderful life-size exhibit of a campground and the animals that you'd find in that setting, including two owl puppets that hide in an artificial tree. In another room, you'll find a few aquariums with animals native to the Houston area such as snakes (yikes!), turtles and fish. Explore at the table of rubber bugs. Check out the child-friendly microscope to examine the smallest creatures. The butterfly exhibit shows visitors the evolution from caterpillar to cocoon to butterfly by illustrating the butterflies you'll see in your backyard. While my daughter is still a bit young for this, she didn't miss a beat with the puppet stage. If only she'd kept the rubber bugs alone! There's also an outdoor sanctuary with a quail, bunnies and more.

Recommended age: 3+ years to foster an understanding of nature

Admission: FREE

Time: T-Sun noon-5:30 pm; Closed M

Physical location: 7112 Newcastle between Bellaire and Beechnut

www.NatureDiscoveryCenter.org

713-667-6550

How would you rate this?

Visit the **Nolan Ryan Center** in Alvin in tribute of a hometown hero. Exhibits show the great pitcher's history from little league baseball through the majors. Youngsters love the pitch-catch exhibit that allows them to experience the feel of catching one of Ryan's pitches. Strollers are not permitted.
Recommended age: 5+ years
Admission: Adults $5; Children $2
Time: T-Sat 9 am–4 pm; Sun noon–4 pm; Closed M
Physical location: Alvin Community College at 2925 South Bypass 35
www.Alvin.cc.tx.us/Ryan/Nolan.htm
281-388-1134

How would you rate this?

Oil Ranch is a fun trip out of the city with so much to do for the entire family. Plan on spending a good part of your day here to allow for the drive and all the activities. With lifeguards provided, the swimming pool is open during the summer through September, so bring your swimsuits. Other activities include pony rides, playing among Indian teepees, touring the lake by train, visiting the petting zoo and much more. You can even hand-milk a cow. Bring water because it's hot outside. Food is available for purchase but it's limited to concession stand fare.
Recommended age: 1+ years
Admission: $9 per person; Discounts are available for groups of 10 or more. You often receive a coupon when you visit so it encourages you to visit again.
Time: 10 am–6 pm
Physical location: #1 Oil Ranch Road in Hockley.

From Houston, head northwest on 610. Take Highway 290 West. Exit Hegar Rd. (Hegar Rd. is approx. 16 miles west of 1960/Hwy. 6 on 290 and 29 miles from the 610 loop). Turn right on Hegar Rd. Go approximately 5 miles and follow the signs to the Oil Ranch.

www.OilRanch.com 281-859-1616

How would you rate this? ☐ ☐

Old MacDonald's Farm is a treat for families that like animals. This farm includes the usual cows, ponies and pigs that you can pet, but it also has peacocks, a wombat and even prairie dogs. That's only naming a few animals in the 12 petting zoo pens here. My daughter adored the train ride around the farm, which is also a great start to your visit because you can see all that the farm has to offer. Old MacDonald's Farm also features several playground areas, a large sand hill with buckets and toys, a fort and an Indian village with a teepee. A swimming pool is on the premises but no lifeguards are on duty. Go early to beat the heat and pack a picnic lunch with cool drinks and popsicles for the kids. (Food and drinks are available for purchase as well.) The best characteristics about this farm are the friendly people and plenty of activities for most ages. Wear athletic shoes and pants or shorts.

Recommended age: 1+ years

Admission: $7 per person; Toddlers under 18 months FREE

Time: 10 am-6 pm March 1-Oct. 31 daily; weekends only in Nov and Feb; Closed Dec.-Jan.

Physical location: 3203 FM 1960 East, Humble (~1 miles north of central Houston)
www.EIEIOHumble.com 281-446-4001

How would you rate this? ☐ ☐

How about a cool way to cheer on good nutrition and fun art? **The Orange Show Monument** is an outdoor 3,000 square foot structure with maze-like design. It includes an oasis, a wishing well, a pond, a stage, a museum, a gift shop, and several upper decks. It is constructed of concrete, brick, steel and found objects including gears, tiles, wagon wheels, mannequins, tractor seats and statuettes. This is a family-fun way to embrace funky art that sings the praises of the orange, the favorite fruit of the monument's creator. When you are short on time but want to do something different with the kids, this is an inexpensive way to conquer that feat.
Recommended age: All
Admission: $1 per adult; kids under 12 are FREE
Time: 9 am-1 pm during the summer weekdays; noon-5 pm weekends year-round
Physical location: 2402 Munger St. (off of I-45 south)
www.OrangeShow.org 713-926-6368

How would you rate this? ☐ ☐

Take a trip to one of Houston's **parks** and enjoy. Pack a ball and cold drinks. One of our favorites is Donovan Park, which takes a clever approach to outdoor fun. The Heights Association hired a skilled architect to design this park with a train theme since an old railroad track is nearby. Huge forts made of heavy-duty wood provide the playground foundation. Slides, swings, bridges and even a wooden locomotive to climb in are creative park features. Colorful tiles contributed by local children decorate the outer perimeter of the park. Pack a lunch or snack and enjoy the outdoors in this fantastic Heights park.

Recommended age: All
Admission: FREE
Time: Dawn to dusk
Physical location: various
For a list of city parks with a map, visit
www.HoustonTx.gov/Parks. *Donovan Park is located at 702 Heights Blvd. at 7th Street and is open dawn to dusk daily. For details, visit*
www.HoustonHeights.org/DonovanPark.htm.

How would you rate this?

The **Planetarium** at the Houston Museum of Natural Science offers a nice break from the norm. Some shows are for more mature audiences, but kids age six and older will enjoy shows such as Legends of the Night Sky: Orion. Unlike IMAX, the Planetarium features shows that are related to the museum's exhibits. Even space shuttle astronauts visit the planetarium for training purposes. Some children are scared once the lights go out, so be sure to reassure your children.

Recommended age: 6-10 years
Admission: Adults $6; children $4
Time: 9 am-9 pm

Physical location: in Houston Museum of Natural Science at One Hermann Circle Dr.
www.HMNS.org 713-639-4629

How would you rate this? ☐ ☐

Many Houstonians seem to overlook the **Port of Houston**, but it's a strength for this city. Take a 1.5 hour tour of the port and you'll gain a new appreciation for it. Weekend tours tend to be less crowded because school groups make a lot of visits on weekdays. Reservations are required.
Recommended age: 3+ years
Admission: FREE
Time: T, W, F and Sat at 10 am and 2:30 pm; Th and Sun 2:30 pm
Physical location: 7300 Clinton Drive
www.PortofHouston.com/SamHou/SamHou.html
713-670-2416

How would you rate this? ☐ ☐

Pump It Up is another option for kids age 3+ years. This entertainer encourages kids to use their energy to have fun by tackling inflatable slides, castles and more. Bounce, slide, crawl and jump. My Goddaughter had her third birthday party here and loved it. Her parents appreciated the easiness of hosting a party there. Don't forget to wear socks.
Recommended age: 3+ years
Admission: $6 per child
Time: M, Th and F 10 am-noon is usually pop-in play time during the school year but call ahead first. Pump It

Up schedules private parties regularly.
Physical locations:
7620 Katy Frwy. in the Marq*E Center 713-686-7867
10910 West Sam Houston Parkway N., Ste 100, in CyFair 281-469-4205
923 S. Mason Rd. in Katy 281-829-5711
23810 Hwy 59 N. in Kingwood 281-359-5515
www.PumpItUpParty.com

How would you rate this? ☐ ☐

Try some putt-putt golf with the family. Five venues are listed below but many are available throughout Houston. Plus, these entertainment centers also offer other games once your little golfer(s) yearns for other activities.
Recommended age: 2+ years

Celebration Station

Admission: Adults $6; Children 5-12 years $4; Children under 5 years free with paying adult
Time: Sun-Th 10 am-10 pm; F-Sat 10 am-11 pm
Physical location: 180 West Rankin Rd., Houston 77090; 281-872-7778
Physical location: 6767 Southwest Freeway, Houston 77074; 713-981-7888
www.CelebrationStation.com

How would you rate this? ☐ ☐

Fast Track Go-Carts

Admission: $5 for 18 holes; go-carts and rides are extra but a coupon is on the Web site.
Time: Sun-Th noon-midnight; F-Sat noon- 2 am; Sun for

private parties only
Physical location: 11440 Hempstead Rd., Houston, TX.
77092
www.HoustonFastTrack.com

How would you rate this? ☐ ☐

Funplex
Admission: Regularly adults $4; children $3.75;
F $0.99 for all
Time: M-Th 10 am-6 pm; F-Sat 10 am-midnight;
Sun noon-9 pm
Physical location: 13700 Beechnut, Houston 77083
www.FunPlex.com 281-530-7777

How would you rate this? ☐ ☐

Mountasia
Admission: Adults $6; children $5; Look for special
discounts.
Physical locations:
Mountasia Houston, 17190 Highway 249, Houston,
TX 77064; 281-894-9791
Time: M–Th 10 am-10 pm; F–Sat 10 am-11 pm; Sun
noon-10 pm

Mountasia Kingwood
26000 Highway 59 North, Kingwood, TX 77339; 281-
359-4653
Time: M-Th 4-9 pm; F 4-11 pm; Sat 11 am-11 pm;
Sun noon–9 pm
www.Mountasia.com

How would you rate this? ☐ ☐

Putting Edge – Glow-in-the-Dark Mini Golf

Admission: 13+ years $8.50; 7-12 years $7.50; 5-6 years and seniors $6; under 4 years free.
Time: Sun-Th 10 am-10 pm; F-Sat 10 am-midnight
Physical location: 7620 Katy Freeway in the Marq-E Entertainment Center
www.PuttingEdge.com 713-263-7051

How would you rate this? ☐ ☐

When the heat is unbearable in Houston, tackle some indoor activity by **roller skating.** The need for balance leads to a hilarious bonding experience for adults and children. Several rinks are around town but our all-time favorite is the **Dairy Ashford Roller Rink**.

In addition to regular skating, the Dairy Ashford Roller Rink offers an awesome **Preschool Skate** program for children six and under (and their parents) every Friday morning from 10 am-noon. This is a fun way to add some humor to your life. Plus, it gets you and your little ones active and out of the house.

Recommended age: 5+ for regular skate; 0-5 years for Preschool Skate
Admission: $4.25 - $5.50, depending on day and time
Time: Closed M; T-F noon-6 pm; Th 6-9 pm; F 6-10:30 pm; Sat noon-5 pm and 5-10:30 pm; Sun 1-5 pm
Physical location: 1820 S Dairy Ashford St.;
www.SkateDARR.com 281-493-5651

How would you rate this? ☐ ☐

Robert Vines Environmental Science Center & Arboretum is a cool place to explore taxidermied animals on display. Wow! This has some neat stuff.

Recommended age: 3+ years
Admission: FREE
Time: Weekdays 8:30 am–5 pm
Physical location: 8856 Westview (near Bingle and I-10)
www.SpringBranchISD.com/instruc/science/vsc/faq.htm
713-365-4175

How would you rate this? ☐ ☐

Native Texans and transplants will enjoy a trip to the **Sam Houston Memorial Museum** north on I-45 in Huntsville. Learn more about Sam Houston, the first president of the Republic of Texas, while looking up at the 67-foot statue of this gentleman.
Recommended age: 5+ years
Admission: FREE
Time: T–Sat 9 am–4:30 pm; Sun noon–4:30 pm
Physical location: corner of Sam Houston Avenue and 19th St. in Huntsville
www.SHSU.edu~smm www 936-294-1832

How would you rate this? ☐ ☐

Head to **Space Center Houston** for activities that are both educational and fun. Young visitors will enjoy the Kids Space Place, which serves as an indoor astronaut playground with lots of hands-on activities. Other astronauts-at-heart will love this place for the tram tours of the Johnson Space

Center, interactive exhibits and more. Allow five hours to take advantage of everything. (Spring, summer and fall feature different children's exhibits so visit again to see the changing displays.).
Recommended age: 3+ years
Admission: Adults $18; Children (age 4-11) $14. See The Houston Chronicle for 50 percent off coupons. Parking is an additional $4.
Time: Weekdays 10 am-5 pm; Weekends 10 am-6 pm; extended holiday hours apply.
Physical location: 1601 NASA Road 1, approximately 25 miles south of downtown Houston in the NASA/Clear Lake area
www.SpaceCenter.org 281-244-2100

How would you rate this? ☐ ☐

Texas Children's Gallery is an artistic way to teach your kids about children fighting cancer. Patients from Texas Children's Hospital as well as other cancer centers have contributed artwork about facing cancer. Take your children here to view the art, but talk to them first about how doctors and nurses help all people overcome medical obstacles. It's important to reassure children so they feel safe while helping them to understand that others may not be as fortunate.
Recommended age: 6+ years
Admission: FREE but parking fees apply.
Time: 24 hours
Physical location: 1101 Bates in the Medical Center
www.ChildCancerPain.org/Gallery.cfm
832-824-1000

How would you rate this? ☐ ☐

When your family is climbing the walls, head to **Texas Rock Gym** and put that energy to good use. For youngsters, top-rope climbing is your best bet. This requires two people: a climber and a belayer. The adult can best serve as the belayer who stays on the ground to operate the safety equipment and keeps the climber's rope taut. This way, if the climber lets go or falls, he/she won't go far. Then, the climber can focus his/her energy on climbing to the top of the mountain. Not only is this fun, but it also teaches kids health, discipline, trust (with the belayer) and confidence. Visits during off-peak hours allow you more time climbing and lower prices. Peak hours are Fridays 3 pm-Sunday 5 pm.

Recommended age: 5+ years

Admission: Prices vary based on location but plan on approximately $24/person.

Time: M, W, Th 10 am-10 pm; T, F, Sat 10 am-11 pm; Sun 9:30 am-8 pm

The Clear Lake location is less expensive but is smaller. A $7.50 student (week)day pass is available only at the Clear Lake location.

Physical location: Memorial location is 1526 Campbell 713-973-7625

Clear Lake location is 201 Hobbs R.D., Suite #A1 in League City 281-338-7625

www.TexRockGym.com

How would you rate this?

Help children learn the importance of giving back to the community. Find a volunteer activity that you enjoy and get your kids involved. As early as three years old, children can understand the importance of helping others. Visit **www.volunteermatch.org** and do an advanced search for great activities or check out the volunteer activities listed on the following pages.

AIDS Foundation Houston, Inc.
Contact: Marc Cohen
713-623-6796

American Diabetes Association
Contact: Ralston Creswell
713-977-7706 x6083

BEAR… Be A Resource for CPS Kids
Contact: Charlotte Pennye
713-695-5149

Museum of Fine Arts
Contact: Lou Palermo
713-639-7749
LPalermo@mfah.org

The Children's Museum of Houston
Contact: Renee Gonzalez
713-522-1138

Reach Out & Read, Texas
Contact: Diane Latson
713-500-3836
Must be age 16 or older; I loved this one.

Sheltering Arms Senior Services
Contact: Joan Arnold
713-667-2840

DePelchin Children's Center
Contact: Wendy Wood
713-802-7792

SPCA
Contact: Julie Knapp
713-869-7722 x129
www.SPCAHouston.org

Holocaust Museum Houston
Contact: Suzanne Sutherland
713-942-8000 x102
Sutherland@hmh.org

The Houston Food Bank
713-547-8609
www.HoustonFoodBank.org

Dress for Success
Contact: Chandra Brooks
713-957-3779

Star of Hope
Contact: Elizabeth Hatler
713-748-0700 x222
Must be age 16 or older

Houston Museum of Natural Science
Contact: David Temple
713-639-4629

M.D. Anderson Cancer Center
Contact: Maggi Suttles
713-792-7180

Memorial Hermann Hospital
www.MemorialHermann.org/Services/
Volunteer.html
Must be age 15 or older
Teen Health Clinic, Baylor College of Medicine
Contact: Peggy B. Smith
713-873-3601
High school seniors only

Texas Children's Hospital
Contact: Pat Dolan
832-824-1000

Wabash Antiques & Feed Store reminds me of a country store with exciting goodies. You'll find lots of fruit, vegetable and spice plants that you can buy and plant in your yard. Walk through the store to see parrots, bunnies, cats, dogs and other animals that you can purchase, too. Even if you don't buy anything, this is a fun way to explore.
Recommended age: 6+ months
Admission: FREE but products vary in price.
Time: M-F 9 am-6 pm; Sat 8:30 am-6 pm; Sun 10 am-5 pm
Physical location: 5701 Washington Avenue, Houston, TX 77007
www.WabashFeed.com 713-863-8322

How would you rate this?

Head to the **Williams Tower & Water Wall** (formerly known as Transco Tower). My daughter loved the noise of the rushing water and the feel of the spraying mist when she ventured toward the center of the waterfall. Make guesses as to how much water there is and why it makes so much noise. This is another great photo op. There's also a nice grassy area in front of the waterfall for kids to run around on. Bring a snack and just chill out.

Visitor parking is available in the nearby parking garage for only $1. Don't waste your time trying to park at the apartments. Just head for the garage.
Recommended age: All
Admission: FREE
Time: Dawn to dusk
Physical location: 2800 Post Oak Blvd. near the Galleria
713-966-7799
How would you rate this?

CHAPTER 3: RESTAURANTS WITH FAMILY APPEAL

The city of Houston has tasty restaurants, but which ones truly welcome families with children? Our family investigated all sorts of restaurants to compile an exhaustive list of places to eat. If the food or service didn't measure up, we did not include the restaurant in this list. The restaurants featured in chapter 3 have tons of family appeal. Try out a new one today and avoid the drive-through window.

To help your family navigate the restaurant scene, each review includes a price rating based on the following legend.

$	very reasonably priced
$$	reasonably priced
$$$	somewhat pricey

Below is a quick overview of restaurants with FREE Kids' Nights. For more details, check out the alphabetical listing of restaurant reviews that follows. As with the activities, times and promotions are subject to change so call ahead to verify the details.

Tuesday:

- Bennigan's offers FREE kids meals 4-10 pm.

- Red Robin Restaurant kicks off kids night from 6:30-8:30 pm. Kids eat FREE and are entertained by a magician, balloon artist and sometimes even the red robin character.

- Boudreaux's Cajun Kitchen invites kids to eat FREE all day Tuesday. No, all the food is not spicy hot.

Wednesday:

- James Coney Island celebrates children each Wednesday after 4 pm.

- Luby's Cafeterias offer FREE kids meals on Wednesdays starting at 4:30 pm.

Saturday:

- Texas Land & Cattle features a Kids Eat FREE promotion from 11 am–4 pm.

Amazon Grill is a good place to grab a bite to eat when you have little mouths to feed, but want a break from the "Just Kids in Mind" mentality. The restaurant is casual so I didn't feel terrible about the food my daughter dropped on the floor. I really liked the relaxed atmosphere and the self-serve salad bar, where you help yourself to plantains, chips, salsa and salad while your meal is being prepared. My fish tacos were delicious and our daughter liked her quesadillas. We were all members of the clean plate club so no complaints on the food.

High chairs are available but no slings for the very little ones. Amazon Grill does have a small kids' menu that's very tasty. I wish they had a coloring page or other kids activity though. Plus, my sister entertained my daughter on the patio while the rest of us finished our dinner.

Physical locations:

5114 Kirby Drive, Houston, TX 77098   713-522-5888
 Hours: M–Th 11 am-10 pm; F 11 am-11 pm;
 Sat 9 am-11 pm; Sun 9 am-9 pm

9600 Westheimer (at Woodlake Square),
 Houston, TX 77063   713-933-0980
 Hours: M-Th 11 am-9 pm; F-Sat 11 am-11 pm; Sun 11 am-9 pm

www. Cordua.com/Cordua.cfm?a=cms,c,8,4

Kid Friendliness: B-
Food Quality: A-
Price: $$

Auntie Pasto's is a cute, small pizzeria with other Italian dishes. A local family owns and operates it as a neighborhood favorite. The kids' menu includes ravioli, chicken fingers, pizza and pasta.

Physical location:
5101 Bellaire Boulevard, Bellaire, TX 77401   713-669-8658
    Hours: M-Th 11 am-10 pm; Fri 11 am-11 pm;
    Sat 4-11 pm; Sun 4-9 pm
Kid Friendliness: B+
Food Quality: A
Price: $$

We visited **Benihana** with a four month old, a five month old, a four year old, a seven year old, and several adults. Everyone had a good time. Not only is the Japanese food tasty, but the chef also prepares the food on a grill built into your table. The kids aren't the only ones who giggle at the sight of flying shrimp and rice popping on the grill. This is fantastic for groups or large/ extended families.

Physical locations:
1318 Louisiana, Houston, TX 77002   713-659-8231
9707 Westheimer, Houston, TX 77042   713-789-4962
    www.Benihana.com

Hours: M-Th 11 am-2:30 pm; 5-9:30 pm; F 11 am-2:30 pm; 5-10:30 pm; Sat 5-10:30 pm; Sun 5-9 pm

Kid Friendliness: A
Food Quality: A
Price: $$-$$$

Bennigan's serves American food with an Irish twist. Kids receive their own menu with coloring activities and end the meal with a clover cookie.

Physical locations:

10690 Northwest Fwy. Houston, TX 77092	713-957-3312
5015 Westheimer Rd., Houston, TX 77056	713-621-3921
3963 Kirby Dr., Houston, TX 77098	713-524-5884
222 North Belt, Houston, TX 77060	281-820-4776
17125 Tomball Pkwy, Houston, TX 77064	281-894-5050
2700 S Loop West, Houston, TX 77054	713-660-7380
12008 E Freeway, Houston, TX 77029	713-453-4008
4505 Fm 1960 West, Houston, TX 77069	281-893-7011
7143 Gulf Freeway, Houston, TX 77087	713-644-9691
211 Fm 1960 West #m, Houston, TX 77090	281-444-1433
140 Fm 1960 E Bypass, Humble, TX 77338	281-446-4646
20210 Katy Fwy., Katy, TX 77449	281-829-1590
11940 Dickinson Rd., Houston, TX 77089	281-481-1779

www.Bennigans.com
Hours: Sun-Th 11 am-midnight; F-Sat 11 am-2 am

Kid friendliness: B+
Food Quality: B
Price: $

Black Eyed Pea has a kids' menu, crayons and activity placemat for children. Parents appreciate the home-style cooking in a friendly environment for the whole family. The vegetables are delicious and yes, they have black-eyed peas. Physical locations:

2675 Wilcrest, Houston TX 77042	713-266-0928
10999 Northwest Fwy., Houston TX 77092	713-681-9500
410 South Mason Rd., Katy TX 77450	281-392-5313
2048 West Gray, Houston TX 77019	713-523-0200
4211 Bellaire, Houston TX 77025	713-661-3642
3434 Fm 1092, Missouri City TX 77459	281-261-0383
10903 Jones Road, Houston TX 77065	281-890-6851
1400 Loop 336 West, Conroe TX 77304	936-760-1709
9710 Fm 1960 Bypass, Humble TX 77338	281-446-3399

www.TheBlackEyedPea.com
Hours: M-F 10:30 am-10 pm; Sat-Sun 11 am-10 pm

Kid Friendliness: A
Food Quality: B+
Price: $$

Boston Market offers kids meals and is very family-friendly. (The $0.99 kids meals were discontinued but the food is still yummy.) We appreciate the variety of vegetables and delicious macaroni. Kids can see the food available and easily decide which they prefer that day. With a slightly smaller selection than most cafeterias, this can be more manageable with youngsters.

Physical locations:

1915 W. Gray St. (near Dunlavy) Houston, TX 77019	713-521-2121
7616 Westheimer (near Voss) Houston, TX 77063	713-780-7995
4672 Beechnut St. Houston, TX 77096	713-667-8800

www.BostonMarket.com
   Hours: 10:30 am-10 pm daily

Kid Friendliness: B+
Food Quality: A
Price: $

Boudreaux's Cajun Kitchen combines fast service with good Cajun food. (Trust me. A quarter of my family lives in Louisiana.) The kids' menu includes shrimp, catfish, chicken, cheeseburgers, grilled cheese, mac 'n cheese and corn dogs. There's also "a video game area" so encourage your child to bring some change or do a chore to earn some game money. Of special note: kids eat FREE all day on Tuesdays.

Physical locations:

5475 West Loop South, Houston, TX 77081
   (near the Galleria)   713-838-2200
100 Gulfgate Center, Houston, TX 77087   713- 643-5000
17595 Tomball Pkwy, Houston, TX 77064   281-469-8500
12806 Gulf Freeway, Houston, TX 77034   281-464-6800
   www.Boudreaux.net
   Hours: Sun-Th 11 am-10 pm; F-Sat 11 am-11 pm

Kid Friendliness: B
Food Quality: A
Price: $$

Buca Di Beppo charms patrons with authentic Italian food served family style, making it a good option for families with kids. The kids' menu includes various pizzas, macaroni and other traditional Italian food for kids age 10 and younger. Call ahead for reservations on the weekend because they fill up quickly.

Physical locations:

5192 Buffalo Speedway at West Park, Houston TX 77005   713-665-2822

19075 Interstate 45 South, Conroe, TX 77385   936-321-6262

www.BucaDiBeppo.com

Hours: M-Th 5-10 pm; F 5-11 pm; Sat 4-11 pm;
Sun noon-2 pm

Kid Friendliness: B
Food Quality: B
Price: $$

Café Adobe is a good outing for both adults and kids. If you like Mexican food, this is a great choice. The food is bueno and we loved how they catered to my daughter. The kids' menu is also a coloring page with activities that comes with three crayons. The waiter brought my daughter a balloon and carefully tied it to her high-chair. When her balloon mysteriously disappeared above our heads, another waitress replaced it with another without a request. The location at the Marqu*e is surrounded by fun activities ranging from Pump It Up! to playing in the fountains and running in the courtyard. Thumbs up on Café Adobe.

Physical locations:

2111 Westheimer Road, Houston, TX 77098   713-528-1468

7620 Katy Fwy., Houston, TX 77024 (at the Marqu*e)   713-688-1700

www.CafeAdobe.com

Hours: Sun-Th 11 am-10 pm; F-Sat 11 am-11 pm

Kid Friendliness: A-
Food Quality: A-
Price: $$

Cazadore's is very good and kid-friendly. I was surprised when a child welcomed our family at the front door. The menu is exceptionally large and includes a kids section. Best of all, this casual restaurant doesn't usually have a wait even on a Friday night.

Physical Location:

11081 NW Freeway, Houston, TX 77092   713-682-2236
    Hours: M-Sat 11 am-10 pm; Sun 11 am – 9 pm

Kid Friendliness: B+
Food Quality: A-
Price: $

Don't be misled by the name. **The Cheesecake Factory** has an extensive menu full of wonderful lunch and dinner dishes. I love the huge salads and the Tex-Mex eggrolls. In fact, the servings are so big, it is easy to share with the kids. Make reservations to avoid a wait. Looking for a good Sunday brunch spot? Look no further. The kids' brunch features french toast, bacon and strawberries. Yum!

Physical locations:

5015 Westheimer (in Galleria) Houston, TX 77056   713-840-0600
1201 Lake Woodlands Dr., Spring, TX 77380   281-419-3400
    www.TheCheesecakeFactory.com
    Hours: M-Th 11 am-11 pm; F-Sat 11 am – 12:30 am;
    Sun 10 am – 11 pm

Kid Friendliness: B
Food Quality: A
Price: $$-$$$

The billboards aren't the only things that are amusing about **ChickFilA**. This restaurant redefines fast food. You can quickly order a kids meal and an adult breakfast, lunch or dinner and be on your way. The waffle fries are worth craving. Counting calories? Try a salad or chicken wrap. The Holcombe location has kids' night on Tuesdays from 5-7 pm with a clown and balloons.

Physical locations:

9800 Hempstead Hwy. in Northwest Mall, Houston, TX 77092	713-680-9172
1200 McKinney Ave., Houston, TX 77010	713-650-8081
5015 Westheimer Rd. at Galleria, Houston, TX 77056	713-840-8810
2715 Southwest Freeway at Kirby, Houston, TX 77098	713-523-2442
5005 Richmond Ave., Houston, TX 77056	713-621-0077
303 Memorial City Way, Houston, TX 77024	713-467-6862
3101 West Holcombe Blvd., Houston, TX 77025-1533	713-660-8200

www.Chick-Fil-a.com
Hours: M-Sat 6:30 am-10 pm; Closed Sun.

Kid Friendliness: A
Food Quality: A-
Price: $

Chili's Grill is another casual restaurant with American and Tex-Mex cuisine. Enjoy the Just for Kids menu with your typical items, plus sides ranging from French fries to cinnamon apples. The queso is delicious.

Physical locations:

3215 Southwest Frwy. Houston, TX 77027	713-592-5100
5015 Westheimer in Galleria, Houston, TX 77056	713-622-7924
10510 Northwest Frwy. at Mangum Houston, TX 77092	713-681-0582

6121 Westheimer Rd., Houston, TX 77057-4523   832-251-0454

10101 S. Post Oak, Houston, TX 77096   713-728-5552

www.Chilis.com

Hours: M-Th 11 am-11 pm; F-Sat 11 am – midnight;
Sun 10:30 am-11 pm

Kid Friendliness: B-
Food Quality: B+
Price: $$

Chuck E. Cheese's is a great option for young boys and girls alike. With indoor facilities, parents don't have to worry about the weather. You'll likely even encounter a visit from Chuck E. Cheese himself. The kids love the arcade games and the indoor play equipment like the pit of balls and winding tunnels. Surprising to me, the young children really enjoyed the musical performance by Chuck E. and friends. It's hilarious to watch the little ones dance. This is a great birthday option for kids age 3+.

Physical locations:

16790 Interstate 45 South, Conroe, TX 77385   936-271-1550

2220 FM 1960, Houston, TX 77090   281-893-2148

6787 Hwy 6 North, Houston, TX 77084   281-550-6500

5535 Weslayan Ave., Houston, TX 77005   713-666-9802

600 Gulfgate Mall Center, Houston, TX 77087   713-645-5660

14637 Memorial Dr., Houston, TX 77079   281-531-7066

6760 Antoine, Houston, TX 77091   713-957-1230

124 E. FM 1960 Bypass, Humble, TX 77338   281-540-1536

5000 Katy Mills Circle, Katy, TX 77494   281-644-4949

154 Fairmont Parkway, Pasadena, TX 77504   713-941-5547

11920 Southwest Frwy., Stafford, TX 77477   281-575-9891

2303 Town Center Drive, Sugar Land, TX 77478   281-277-3283

1541 West Bay Area Blvd., Webster, TX 77598   281-332-9780

www.ChuckECheese.com

Hours vary but are usually Sun-Th 9 am-10 pm;
F-Sat 9 am-11 pm.

Kid Friendliness: A+
Food Quality: C
Price: $$

Chuy's adds a fun twist to Mexican food. This restaurant pays tribute to Elvis Presley by featuring art and decorations of the King. The kids' menu makes it easy to order for smaller mouths. The festive atmosphere allows kids to be somewhat vocal without disrupting other patrons. The outdoor patio is great when it's not too hot outside. Visitors will usually encounter a long wait on Friday nights. For an extra fun dining experience, head to Chuy's for the Annual Green Chile Festival in August and September, when they have giveaways and turn up the festivities.

Physical location:

2706 Westheimer at Kirby, Houston, TX 77098   713-524-1700

www.Chuys.com

Hours: Sun-Th 11 am-11 pm; F-Sat 11 am—midnight

Kid Friendliness: B
Food Quality: A-
Price: $$

Ci-Ci's Pizza offers inexpensive pizza and pasta for families. Walk through the buffet line to select from 16 types of pizza. For only $4.50, you can enjoy the all-you-can-eat buffet of pizza, pasta, salad and dessert. This is a good place to dine after the kids' ball game or other extracurricular activity.

Physical locations:

4400 N. Fwy., Ste 300-A, Houston, TX 77022	713-691-2444
200 Northwest Mall, Houston, TX 77092	713-682-1616
5911 Bellaire Blvd, Houston, TX 77401	713-667-9700
814 South 75th, Houston, TX 77023	713-923-7707
10601 S. Post Oak, Houston, TX 77035	713-721-0017
8366 Westheimer, Houston, TX 7706	713-789-0004
11410 I-10 East, Suite 150, Houston, TX 77029	713-455-8845
7441 W. Tidwell, Houston, TX 77040	713-690-2229
6119 Telephone Rd., Houston, TX 77087	713-649-8117
1037 N. Gessner, Houston, TX 77055	713-464-0499

www.CiCisPizza.com

Hours: Sun-Th 11 am-10 pm; F-Sat 11 am-11 pm

Kid Friendliness: A
Food Quality: B
Price: $

Clay's Restaurant gets a thumbs up for family-friendliness. This casual country joint serves burgers, salads and sandwiches. Your typical kids' menu offers corn dogs, grilled cheese, popcorn shrimp, etc. While parents enjoy a frosty beverage like a frozen margarita, kids lap up their own blue frozen concoction. No worries. It's just blue punch. What separates this restaurant from the others is its large outdoor area. Kids love looking at the horses, donkey, ducks, goats, sheep and turkey. This really adds to the authenticity of the joint. A covered sand pit with toys also keeps the kids busy, while the adults finish their meals and conversation. There's also an arcade room in the back for indoor fun.

Physical location:

17715 Clay Road near Hwy. 6, Houston, TX 77084   281-859-3773

     Hours: M-Th 11 am-9 pm; F-Sat 11 am-10 pm

Kid Friendliness: A+

Food Quality: B+

Price: $

Cliff's Hamburgers serves juicy burgers and fries for Houston families. You'll move through the ordering line quickly and be eating in no time. Kids enjoy burgers or chicken tenders. Check out the breakfast, too.

Physical locations:

12389 Kingsride Lane, Houston, TX 77024	713-647-7466
6202 Highway 6 South, Houston, TX 77083	281-879-8024
1822 Fountain View Drive, Houston, TX 77057	713-780-4010
12102 Westheimer Rd, Houston, TX 77077	281-558-3371
3333 Fm 1960 Road West, Houston, TX 77068	281-580-0127

     www.CliffsHamburgers.com

     Hours: M-Sat 7 am-7 pm; Sun 7 am-3 pm

Kid Friendliness: B+

Food Quality: B+

Price: $

Collina's Italian Café is oh, so good, but only works with kids old enough to sit still without entertainment. There's no kids' menu but the staff will recommend a personal, eight inch pizza. I love the Chicken Picata. These are casual neighborhood restaurants with good Italian food.

Physical locations:

502 19th Street in the Heights, Houston, TX 77008   713-869-0492

12311 Kingsride, Houston, TX 77024   713-365-9497

3835 Richmond Avenue, Houston, TX 77027   713 621-8844

www.Collinas.com
Hours: M-Th 11 am-10 pm; F-Sat 11 am-11 pm

Kid Friendliness: B-
Food Quality: A
Price: $$

Dave and Buster's combines food and fun in its indoor venue from bowling to arcade games. This is best for kids in elementary school and up. The menu ranges from steak, pasta and seafood to burgers and sandwiches. After your meal, your family can tackle a game of shuffleboard or the arcade.

Physical location:

6010 Richmond at Fountainview, Houston, TX 77057   713-952-2233

www.DaveandBusters.com
Hours: Sun-W 11:30 am-midnight; Th 11:30 am-1 am;
F-Sat 11:30 am-2 am

Kid Friendliness: A
Food Quality: B
Price: $$-$$$

My dad believes the best pizza in town can be found at **Doyle's** on 34th Street. This old-fashioned, casual restaurant has been serving Houstonians since 1954. With one visit, you'll know why it's still here. Our family often shows up with four generations of Houstonians to enjoy Italian pizza, poor boys and baked chicken dishes. You may even see Houston celebrities eating here such as channel 13's Marvin Zindler. Besides serving delicious food, the staff goes the extra mile to make your smile. For youngsters, this restaurant has bibs and high chairs. Your waitress will happily deliver a small dish of fruit for your little one. Our daughter loves the bread, not to mention the pizza. An added bonus is the pick-up window. Call in your order and pick it up for a yummy meal at home.

Physical Location:

2136 West 34th St., Houston, TX 77018   713-686-8271

Hours: M–Sat 10:30 am–8 pm; Closed Sun

Kid Friendliness: A-
Food Quality: A
Price: $$

Epicure Bakery brings European eating to Houston. It's a slower pace restaurant than similar ones. Classical music plays in the background. The kids' menu offers pasta dishes, grilled cheese and other sandwiches with plenty to take home. Adults enjoy baked salmon or chicken, omelettes, soups and salads. For dessert, kids can choose from six to eight flavors of ice cream or enjoy one of the fresh-baked pastries on display. After dinner, enjoy a stroll by the nearby shops. Avoid dinner with kids during peak movie times because River Oaks Movie Theater attendees stop in for a bite to eat before and after shows, causing crowds in this café.

Physical location:

2005 West Gray, Houston, TX 77019   713-520-6174

    Hours: M-Th 8 am-8 pm; F-Sat 8 am-10:30 pm;
    Sun 8 am-7:30 pm

Kid Friendliness: B
Food Quality: B+
Price: $$

Farrago: International fusion cuisine is served at this inviting downtown restaurant. The hostess and waiters went out of their way to keep our daughter content. For instance, the waitress quickly brought our little one fresh fruit and a strawberry muffin to nibble on while the adults perused the menu. The wait staff seemed genuinely pleased that our child paid them a visit, which makes a parent's meal more relaxed. Brunch was delicious and the crowd was lively and pleasant. Try the breakfast quesadilla. A small park across the street is also a good way to burn off some energy. It includes a water fountain that our daughter loved.

While this restaurant is on the southwest side of downtown, this would be a great place to take the family before a play or musical in the theatre district. (It's also a cool place for a parents-night out.)

Physical location:

318 Gray in Midtown, Houston, TX 77002   713-523-6404
   www.Farrago.tv
   Hours: M-W 11 am-10 pm; Th-F 11 am-11 pm;
   Sat brunch 11 am-3 pm and dinner 6-11 pm;
   Sun brunch 11 am-3 pm

Kid Friendliness: B+
Food Quality: A
Price: $$-$$$

The Flying Dutchman Oyster Bar and Patio at the Kemah Boardwalk offers a casual lunch with a view of the bay. The food is good and the kids' menu includes coloring activities. The playground is nearby and handy. The service was slow but friendly.

Physical Location:

Bradford and 2nd Street, Kemah, TX. 77565   281-334-7575

   www.KemahBoardwalk.com Select "restaurants" from menu bar.

   Hours: Sun–Th 11 am–10 pm; F–Sat 11 am–11 pm

Kid Friendliness: A
Food Quality: B
Price: $$

Get your favorite type of pizza in a festive atmosphere at **The Flying Pig**. The restaurant is decorated with pigs flying through the air so it's hard not to be entertained. The kitchen is somewhat viewable, allowing children to watch chefs hand-tossing pizza dough. The service promises to be friendly and the food tasty.

Physical location:

5311 Weslayan near Bissonnet   713-666-3008

   www.LocalConcepts.net

   Hours: Sun-Th 11 am-9 pm; F-Sat 11 am-10 pm

Kid Friendliness: A
Food Quality: A
Price: $

Fuddrucker's allows your little ones to make their hamburgers just the way they like 'em. The kids' meals offers plenty of options and includes a cookie and a choice of French fries, fruit, beans or cole slaw. If your family still has room, share a float, shake or malt. Yummy!

Physical Locations:

111 North 23rd Street in Galveston, TX 77550	409-765-8000
13010 N.W. Frwy., Houston, TX 77040	713-462-4508
7250 Highway 6 North, Houston, TX 77095	281-550-5100
3929 Southwest Frwy., Houston, TX 77027	713-621-8222
7511 FM 1960 West, Houston, TX 77070	281-469-6476
403 Greens Road, Houston, TX 77060	281-876-2611
855 Normandy, Houston, TX 77015	713-453-0672
2475 Kirkwood, Houston, TX 77077	281-496-4490
11950 Kurland, Houston, TX 77034	81-484-7371
3301 FM 1960 West, Houston, TX 77068	281-586-8791
10500 Town & Country Way, Houston, TX 77024	713-722-7440
25407 Bell Patna Dr., Katy, TX 77492	281-644-7616
4360 Kingwood Dr., Kingwood, TX 77339	281-361-7800
2040 Nasa Road One, Nassau Bay, TX 77058	281-333-1598
3149 Silverlake Village Dr., Pearland, TX 77584	713-436-8760
11445 Fountain Lake Dr., Stafford, TX 77477	281-240-9414
2290 Buckthorne Place, The Woodlands, TX 77380	281-367-1343

www.Fuddruckers.com

Hours: M-Th 11 am-10 pm; F-Sat 11 am-10:30 pm; Sun 11 am-10 pm

Kid Friendliness: A
Food Quality: A
Price: $$

Fu's Garden serves Chinese food worth noticing. There's no kids' menu but children are welcome. Take turns reading your fortune from your fortune cookie. Giggles are guaranteed.

Physical locations:

2539 University Boulevard, Houston, TX 77005   713-520-7422

4720 Richmond Avenue, Houston, TX 77027   713-961-7330

5866 San Felipe Street, Houston, TX 77057   713-783-4419
     Hours: Sun-Th 11 am-10 pm; F-Sat 11:30 am-10:30 pm

Kid Friendliness: C+
Food: A
Price: $$

Gatti Town is similar to Chuck E. Cheese's but better for older children and adults. Not only does it have the typical arcade games, but it also includes bumper cars, a carousel, shooting gallery and a rock wall. This is an alcohol-free, smoke-free environment.

Physical location:

1475 FM 1960 Bypass in Humble   281-446-PRTY (7789)
     www.HumbleGattiTown.com
     Hours: Sun–Th 11 am-10 pm but the buffet closes at 9 pm; F–Sat 11 am-11 pm with the buffet closing at 10 pm

Kid Friendliness: A+
Food Quality: B-
Price: $$-$$$

Goode Company Taqueria and Burgers is casual and yummy. I love the fajitas and queso. Order at the counter and then kick back until your order is called. This is a good weekender. Be sure to check out the weekend breakfasts, served from 7:30 am-12:30 pm.

Physical location:

4902 Kirby Dr., Houston, TX 77098   713-520-9153
    Hours: M-F 11 am-10 pm; Sat-Sun 7:30 am-10 pm

Kid Friendliness: B+
Food Quality: A-
Price: $$-$$$

Lots of folks visit the **Hard Rock Café** when they visit other towns, but don't forget Houston has one of its own. This is also a good birthday hot spot for preteens and teens. After ordering anything from a burger to salmon or pasta, peruse the collection of rock 'n roll memorabilia. The Houston Café has cool stuff like a black boa donated by Gwen Stefani of the band No Doubt, Elvis Presley's blue jacket, Elton John's Statue of Liberty costume, and plenty more. In the midst of downtown, it's easy to spend the evening here.

Physical location:

502 Texas Avenue in the Bayou Place complex downtown 713-227-1392
    www.HardRockCafe.com/locations/cafes
    Hours: Sun-Th 11 am-11 pm; Fri-Sat 11 am-midnight

Kid Friendliness: B
Food Quality: A-
Price: $$$

Grab some grilled burgers at the **Houston Zoo**. Enjoy a relaxing lunch or dinner with your family with a meal behind the food court by the duck pond. And, yes, adults can even cool off with an adult beverage or two.

Physical location:

1513 N MacGregor Dr., Houston, TX 77030   713-533-6500
   www.HoustonZoo.org
   Hours: 9 am-5 pm daily

Kid Friendliness: A
Food Quality: B
Price: $$

You thought Ikea only offered smart shopping? The **Ikea Cafeteria** is a novel idea for families trying to pick up a few necessities but need a bite to eat. The food is a bit bland but is much appreciated. There is a play area with simple toys for the children or you can drop the little ones off at on-site babysitting while you run your errands in the store. Plus, from 9-11 am daily, you can get a good breakfast for only $0.99 each.

Physical location:

7810 Katy Frwy at Antoine, Houston, TX 77024   713-688-7867
   www.ikea.com

Kid Friendliness: A
Food Quality: C+ (Bland but novel)
Price: $

You can tell a *real* Houstonian based on his/her thoughts about **James Coney Island**. My dad took me on "dates" as a child here and I've never forgotten it. I can place my order of one chili cheese Coney, cheese fries and a Delaware Punch in five seconds flat. Stop by one of these restaurants soon and you'll know why. Kids age 10 and younger eat FREE on Wednesdays 4 pm-close.

Physical locations:

1211 Upland Drive, Houston, TX 77043	713-467-2845
530 Meyerland Plaza Mall, Houston, TX 77096	713-664-4900
1109 Bay Area Boulevard, Houston, TX 77058	281-286-7600
1142 Travis Street, Houston, TX 77002	713-652-3819
2020 Highway 6 South, Houston, TX 77077	281-597-0400
12500 East Freeway, Houston, TX 77015	713-451-2550
101 Fm 1960 Road West, Houston, TX 77090	281-893-8455
6955 Gulf Freeway, Houston, TX 77087	713-643-0998
701 Town And Country Blvd., Houston, TX 77024	713-973-9143
3607 South Shepherd Drive, Houston, TX 77098	713-524-7400
10600 Gulf Freeway, Houston, TX 77034	713-944-8980
4200 North Freeway, Houston, TX 77022	713-694-5336
6614 Highway 6 North, Houston, TX 77084	281-345-8768
5745 Westheimer Road, Houston, TX 77057	713-785-9333
5730 Hollister Street, Houston, TX 77040	713-690-8332
740 S. Mason Rd., Katy, TX 77450	281-395-4555
9813 FM 1960, Humble, TX 77338	281-540-8333
3803 Spencer Hwy., Pasadena, TX 77504	713-910-0710
521 Sawdust Rd., Spring, TX 77380	281-298-1556
2127 W. Davis, Conroe, TX 77304	936-441-5070

www.JamesConeyIsland.com
Hours: 10:30 am-9 pm

Kid Friendliness: A
Food Quality: A
Price: $

Jason's Deli allows families to choose from a variety of soups, salads, baked potatoes and sandwiches. End the meal with FREE soft-serve ice cream.

Physical locations:

7010 Highway 6 North, Houston, TX 77095	281-858-7500
10321 Katy Freeway, Houston, TX 77024	713-467-2007
901 McKinney Street, Houston, TX 77002	713-650-1500
5860 Westheimer Road, Houston, TX 77057	713-975-7878
14604 Memorial Drive, Houston, TX 77079	281-531-1999
2530 University Boulevard, Houston, TX 77005	713-522-2660
2611 South Shepherd Drive, Houston, TX 77098	713-520-6728
10915 Fm 1960 Road West, Houston, TX 77070	281-970-5044
5403 Fm 1960 Road West, Houston, TX 77069	281-444-7515
5215 West 34th Street, Houston, TX 77092	713-956-0122

www.JasonsDeli.com
Hours: M-Sat 10 am-9 pm; Closed Sun

Kid Friendliness: A-
Food Quality: A-
Price: $$

Jenni's Noodle House comes highly recommended for pasta with an Asian flair. When we walk in, they ask us if we want them to whip up a little plate with butter, noodles and chicken for the kids along with some dumplings. It is all made fresh so you don't have to worry about food allergies because they know what is in everything. The food is fast and excellent. Our little one loves the butter noodles and wontons.

Physical location:

2130 Jefferson at Hutchins, Houston, TX 77003	713-228-3400

www.NoodlesRule.com
Hours: M-Th 11 am-9 pm; F-Sat 11 am-10 pm

Kid Friendliness: B+
Food Quality A
Price: $$

Joe's Crab Shack has several locations around town with seafood for young and old. This is an inexpensive way to enjoy seafood while keeping your children entertained. Joe's has a great patio play area, if you eat on the deck. The kids' menu and coloring activities keep little ones focused at the table. The fun atmosphere with lots of singing by the wait staff will bring smiles to your family.

Physical locations:

12910 Northwest Fwy., Houston, TX 77040	713-690-8835
2621 South Loop West, Houston, TX 77054	713-666-2150
6218 Richmond, Houston, TX 77057	713-952-5400
17111 Tomball Pkwy., Houston, TX 77064	832-912-1094
14901 North Freeway I-45, Houston, TX 77090	281-875-5400
11900 I-10 East, Houston, TX 77029	713-453-2100
2120 South Highway 6, Houston, TX 77077	281-558-7111

www.JoesCrabShack.com

Kid Friendliness: A
Food Quality: B-
Price: $$

Juanita's Mexican Restaurant offers delicious Mexican food and is easy to get into on Friday night. It may not be healthy, but it's delicious.

Physical location:

2728 W T C Jester Blvd., Houston, TX 77018   713-680-8011
    Hours: M-Sat 11 am-10 pm; Sun 11 am-9 pm

Food: A
Kid Friendliness: A
Price: $$

If your little lady is craving tea and a fresh lunch, **Lords and Ladies Tea Room** is perfect. This restaurant and bookstore are owned and operated by a home schooling family with nine children so they understand kids' needs and wants. Be sure to try one of the various teas and some scones for dessert. There's also a play area for young children while moms shop in the bookstore. Reservations only required for groups of 6 or more.

Physical location:

2020 S Fry Road, Suite E, Katy, TX 77450   281-579-0033
    www.BooksOnThePath.com/katytexasstore.aspx
    Hours: Closed Sun-M; T-Sat 8:30-10 am for breakfast, lunch 11 am-4 pm;

Kid Friendliness: A+
Food Quality: A
Price: $$

Luby's Cafeteria is always good for some home cooking when you don't have the time or inclination to cook. And this cafeteria makes it easy to feed the whole family. The price is right and the options great. The kids' packs supply children with crayons and balloons to keep them occupied while the adults finish their meals. Some locations even have a weekend breakfast buffet.

Physical locations:

12405 East Freeway, Houston, TX 77015	713-455-9998
11595 Fuqua, Houston, TX 77034	281-481-9712
8440 Gulf Freeway, Houston, TX 77017	713-644-1523
1727 Old Spanish Trail, Houston, TX 77054	713-797-0078
2400 South MacGregor Way, Houston, TX 77021	713-747-1771
6223 Bellaire Boulevard, Houston, TX 77081	713-771-4459
1725 Post Oak Blvd., Houston, TX 77056	713-622-1713
12121 Westheimer Road, Houston, TX 77077	281-531-4707
2730 Fondren Road, Houston, TX 77063	713-785-5240
9797 South Post Oak Road, Houston, TX 77096	713-728-4841
1414 Waugh Drive, Houston, TX 77019	713-528-0880
825 Town & Country, Houston, TX 77024	713-461-9404
4518 Hwy 6 North at Aspenglen, Houston, TX 77084	281-859-5134
13451 Northwest Freeway, Houston, TX 77040	713-460-4949
11250 Northwest Freeway, Houston, TX 77092	713-688-7056
7933 Veterans Memorial Drive, Houston, TX 77088	281-820-6594
108 West Greens Road, Houston, TX 77067	281-873-0820
730 West FM 1960, Houston, TX 77090	281-440-5692
4511 FM 1960 West, Houston, TX 77069	281-397-0338
8801 North Loop East, Houston, TX 77029	713-673-2691
5335 Gulf Freeway, Houston, TX 77023	713-928-2221
4709 Center Street, Deer Park, TX 77536	281-479-0067
1014 Baybrook Mall, Houston, TX 77546	281-486-9841
20131 Hwy 59 North, Humble, TX 77338	281-446-0977
485 South Mason Road, Katy, TX 77450	281-492-2016
24004 Highway 59, Kingwood, TX 77339	281-359-6180
1210 East Southmore, Pasadena, TX 77502	713-477-2050
10575 West Airport Blvd., Stafford, TX 77477	281-568-0931
3434 Highway 6 South, Sugar Land, TX 77478	281-980-1696

922 Lake Front Circle, The Woodlands, TX 77380   281-367-7892

1600 Nasa Road One, Houston, TX 77058   281-335-8400

28750 Tomball Parkway, Tomball, TX 7737   281-255-3725

19668 Northwest Freeway, Houston, TX 77065   281-897-0032

11743 Eastex Freeway, Houston, TX 77039   281-590-4336

    www.Lubys.com

    Hours: vary upon location but in general are
    M-Sat 11 am-2:30 pm and 4:15-8 pm; Sun 11 am-8 pm

Kid Friendliness: A

Food Quality: B-

Price: $

Lupe Tortilla's brings Tex-Mex to families and does it well. Kids love the sandy play area with slides, shovels and other toys. Parents should be ready to play in the sand. (Flips flops are extra handy in the sand area.) There's a great kids' menu, too. Parents enjoy the relaxed atmosphere and good food. I recommend a visit on Sunday for lunch to beat the crowd.

Physical locations:

318 Stafford (I-10 at Hwy. 6), Houston, TX 77079   281-496-7580

    M-F Lunch 11 am-2 pm; M-Th 5:30 pm–9 pm;
    F 5:30 pm–10 pm; Sat 11:30 am-10 pm; Sun 11:30 am –9 pm

15315 North Freeway at Richey Rd, Houston, TX 77090   281-873-6220

    Sun-Th 11 am–9 pm; F-Sat 11 am-10 pm

891 W Bay Area Blvd. (East of I-45 South),

    Houston, TX 77598   281-338-2711

    Sun-Th 11 am–9 pm; F-Sat 11 am-10 pm

15801 Southwest Freeway (at Hwy 6 & 59),

    Houston, TX 77478   281-265-7500

    Sun-Th 11 am–9 pm; F-Sat 11 am-10 pm

2414 Southwest Frwy. (near Kirby), Houston, TX 77098   713-522-4420

Sun-Th 11 am-9 pm; F-Sat 11 am-10 pm

22465 Tomball Parkway, Houston, TX 77070   832-843-0004
or 713-559-0180

Sun-Th 11 am–9 pm; F-Sat 11 am-10 pm
www.LupeTortilla.com

Kid Friendliness: A
Food Quality: A
Price: $$

The Mission Burritos on Durham at I-10 has a nice outside area with a small playground and toys. A pint-sized picnic table is available for the kids to eat their meals. The food is fast and tasty. The kids menu offers food just the right size for little mouths and hands, while the main menu offers fresh fast food for adults that beats most fast food establishments… hands down.

Physical locations:

2245 W. Alabama, Houston, TX 77098   713-529-0535
M–F 11 am–10 pm; Sat-Sun 7:30 am-10 pm

1609 Durham, Houston, TX 77007   713-426-6634
M-F 11 am-10 pm; Sat 11 am-10 pm; Sun 11 am-9 pm
www.MissionBurritos.com

Kid Friendliness: A
Food Quality: A
Price: $

Papa Joes' BBQ offers traditional barbeque fare and has kids menus. Management is considering adding a promotion where children receive a FREE toy with the purchase of a meal. Let them know what you think.

Physical location:

12310 Kingsride Lane (near Memorial City Mall),

Houston, TX 77024   713-973-3948

Hours: M-Sat 11 am-8 pm; Closed Sun

Kid Friendliness: B-
Food Quality: B
Price: $$

Thank you to my friend Dan for introducing our family to **Paulie's**. This restaurant is super for kids. Besides a kids' menu, it has a buffet for kids to see and select their food of choice and it includes unlimited visits. My nephew tried cheese pizza and pasta, while my daughter had fruit, a vegetable medley and another pasta with red sauce. There's also grilled chicken, grilled cheese, etc. Paulie's passed the true test for our family: not only was the staff completely accommodating and kid-friendly, but the food was also delicious. My husband and I both chose the $13 fettucine alfredo with chicken breast and two pieces of bread. We should have split it but the next day's leftovers were a treat. Don't forget to leave room for dessert. My sister loved the gooey chocolate chip cookie. The kids liked the dinosaur-shaped shortbread cookies. Paulie's is now a family favorite.

Physical locations:

2617 West Holcombe, Houston, TX 77025   713-660-7057

M–Sat 11 am-9 pm; Sun 11 am-8 pm

1834 Westheimer Rd., Houston, TX 77098   713-807-7271

M–Sat 11 am-9 pm; Closed Sun

www.PauliesCookies.com

Kid Friendliness: A
Food Quality: A
Price: $$

Try **Le Peep** for breakfast or lunch. We loved this. The staff is so friendly. The kids' menu also includes activities and crayons. I was pleasantly surprised at the variety in the menu, too. Most of all, we appreciated our waitress understanding what it's like to be little. She even encouraged our daughter to enjoy herself. Ahh.

Physical locations:

3810 Farnham St. near Shepherd and Hwy. 59, Houston, TX 77098	713-520-5201
6128 Village Parkway, Houston, TX 77005	713-523-7337
11199 Westheimer, Houston, TX 77042	713-789-7337
9801 Katy Frwy. at Memorial City, Houston, TX 77024	713-468-0030
4702 Westheimer, Houston, TX 77027	713-629-7337

> **www.LePeepHouston.com**
> Hours: M-F 6:30 am-2:30 pm; weekends 7 am-2:30 or 3 pm (depending on location)

Kid Friendliness: A
Food Quality: A
Price: $$

Pei Wei is the fast food, order-at-the-counter version of P.F. Changs, but the staff delivers the food to your table. This Asian food eatery includes a kids' menu with a few options for children age 12 and younger for only $3.95, including a drink and fortune cookies. The kids' menu is small but tasty indeed. A plastic cup and straw made it easy sipping for my daughter. The food is great and it is served quickly.

Extra cool things for kids: Pei Wei also has "fun sticks" which are pint-sized chop sticks to help youngsters give Asian eating a real effort. The staff was very accommodating, which always makes parents breathe easier. The restaurant had both high chairs and infant carrier slings, which is important for the Houston families with little babies. This restaurant boasts lively conversation that's not overbearing but works with a talkative youngster. Plus, the manager was on site to greet my daughter and wave good-bye to her.

Physical locations:

5110 Buffalo Speedway, Houston, TX 77005	713-661-0900
1005 Waugh Street, Houston, TX 77019	713-353-7366
5203 FM 1960 West, Houston, TX 77069	281- 885-5430
19411 - A Gulf Freeway, Webster, TX 77598	281- 554-9876
1590 S Mason Road, Katy, TX 77450	281-392-1410
702 Kingwood Drive, Kingwood, TX 77339	281- 318-2877
14008 Memorial Drive at Kirkwood, Houston, TX 77079	281- 506-3500
19075 I.H. 45 South, Shenandoah, TX 77385	936-321-1153
16101 Kensington Dr., Sugar Land, TX 77479	281-240-1931
12020 FM 1960 West, Houston, TX 77065	281-571-4990

www.PeiWei.com

Hours vary slightly. Sun-Th 11 am–9 pm; F-Sat 11 am-10 pm

Kid Friendliness: B+

Food: A

Price: $

Your children will love the play area and small climbing structure at **Pollo Campero**. The adults will appreciate the good Guatemalan food. Kids' meals include a chicken drumstick, fries, a drink and ice cream. Be sure to try the breakfasts, too.

Physical location:

5616 Bellaire Blvd., Houston, TX 77081	713-395-0990

Hours: 7 am-11 pm daily

Kid Friendliness: A
Food Quality: A
Price: $$

A local family owns **Pronto Cucinino,** an Italian fast casual restaurant. Order at the counter and the servers bring your food to your table. This place is loud enough that baby cries or kid yelps won't cause a disturbance; yet adults can still hold a conversation. Grab a table on the patio, where your children will have room to frolic by the fountain. Our daughter likes the pizza squares and mashed potatoes, but pasta is also a kid favorite.

Physical location:

1401 Montrose (between W. Gray and W. Dallas),

Houston, TX 77019   713-528-TOGO (8646)
www.Pront-2-go.com
Hours: 10:30 am-9 pm daily

Kid Friendliness: B
Food Quality: A
Price: $$-$$$

Quin Dynasty offers fine Chinese cuisine in an authentic atmosphere. While there's not a kids' menu, help your children choose from the selection of appetizers or a rice or noodle dish for the right size meal.

Physical location:

5115 Buffalo Speedway near Westpark,

Houston, TX 77005   713-660-8386

www.QinDynasty.biz
   Hours: Sun-Th 11 am-10 pm; F-Sat 11 am-11 pm

Kid Friendliness: B
Food Quality: A
Price: $

Take a break from the norm and visit the **Rainforest Café**. It's so fun for kids. Wednesday nights are family nights with discounted kids' meals, family entertainment and visits from the rainforest characters. Any day of the week, this restaurant kicks fun up a notch. Every 30 minutes the restaurant experiences an artificial rain show with thunder and lightning that lasts about two minutes. Be sure to explain this to your child before coming so they aren't startled. After dinner, walk through the restaurant to see the exhibits of animals native to rainforests, including the elephants, gorillas and beautiful fish.

Physical locations:

5000 Katy Mills Circle at Katy Mills Dr., Katy, TX 77494   281-644-6200

53rd and the Seawall, Galveston, TX 77551   409-744-6000
   www.RainForestCafe.com
   Hours: M-Th 11 am-9:30 pm; F-Sat 11 am-10 pm;
   Sun 11 am-7:30 pm

Kid Friendliness: A
Food Quality: B+
Price: $$

Tuesday night is kid night at **Red Robin Restaurant**, featuring face painting, balloons and more. The Red Robin character also stops by at the Richmond location. Take home your own cup, color a masterpiece at the table and wrack up some points on your favorite video game. This is good for toddlers as well as older kids.

Physical locations:

10465 Richmond Avenue near Beltway 8,
    Houston, TX 77042   713-783-0900
    Hours: Sun-Th 11 am-10 pm; F-Sat 11 am-11 pm
7620 Katy Freeway at Silber, Houston, TX 77024   713-476-9096
    Hours: Sun-Th 11 am-11 pm; F-Sat 11 am-midnight
    www.RedRobin.com
    Hours: Sun-Th 11 am-11 pm;

Kid Friendliness: A
Food Quality: B
Price: $$

Romano's Macaroni Grill: With more than 35 Italian dishes, you're sure to find a new favorite. The kids' menu offers smaller portions of the parents' meals.

Physical locations:

7607 FM 1960, Houston, TX 77070-5701   281-955-1388
5802 Westheimer, Houston, TX 77057   713-789-5515
1155 Lake Woodlands Dr., The Woodlands, TX 77380 281-367-3773
    www.MacaroniGrill.com
    Hours: Mon-Th 11 am-10 pm; F-Sat 11 am-11 pm;
    Sun 11 am-9 pm
Kid Friendliness: B
Food Quality: B
Price: $$

Skeeter's serves great burgers, salads, burritos and fajitas. And don't forget the weekend breakfast buffet. This is a very family-oriented restaurant that's often filled with local scouts or ball teams.

Physical locations:

5529 Weslayan, Houston, TX 77005	713-660-7090
16535 Lexington, Sugar Land, TX 77479	281-980-0066
700 Town & Country Blvd., Houston, TX 77024	713-461-9773
4747 Research Forest, Spring, TX 77381	281-364-1094
750 Gulfgate Mall, Houston, TX 77087	713-645-9280
1553 S. Mason Rd., Katy, TX 77450	281-398-9260
4121 W. Lake Houston, Houston, TX 77339	281-361-7168
5716 Fairmont Pkwy, Pasadena, TX 77505	281-998-9595
16580 El Camino Real, Houston, TX 77062	281-488-5808
19710 Northwest Frwy., Houston, TX 77065	281-970-8235

www.LocalConcepts.com
Hours vary but usually are M-F 11 am-10 pm; Sat 8 am-10 pm; Sun 8 am-9 pm

Kid Friendliness: A
Food Quality: A-
Price: $$

Souper Salad offers a wide variety of foods from salad to soups to pizza and more. Eating here is fast and the kids love the ice cream dessert. Plus, kids eat for $0.99 on Sundays.

Physical locations:

1574 West Gray, Houston, TX 77019	713-524-3536

Hours: M-Th 10:30 am-9:30 pm; F-Sat 10:30 am-10 pm; Sun 11 am- 8:30 pm

6783 Highway 6 North, Houston TX 77084   281-345-4770
  Hours: M-Th 10:30 am-9:30 pm; F-Sat 10:30 am-10 pm;
  Sun 11 am- 8:30 pm

5460 Weslayan, Houston, TX 77056   713-660-8950
  Hours: M-Th 10:30 am-9:30 pm; F 10:30 am-9 pm;
  Sat 10:30 am-midnight; Sun 11 am- 8:30 pm

10985 Northwest Freeway, Houston, TX 77092   713-957-3498
  Hours: M-Th 10:30 am-9:30 pm; F-Sat 10:30 am-10 pm;
  Sun 11 am- 8:30 pm

6516 Westheimer, Houston, TX 77057   713-785-0536
  Hours: M-Th 10:30 am-9 pm; F-Sat 10:30 am-9 pm;
  Sun 11 am-8:30 pm

4884 Beechnut St., Houston, TX 77096   713-664-4992
  Hours: M-Th 10:30 am-9:30 pm; F-Sat 10:30 am-10 pm;
  Sun 11 am- 8:30 pm

2356 South Hwy 6, Houston, TX 77077   281-556-8097
  Hours: M-Th 10:30 am-9:30 pm; F-Sat 10:30 am-10 pm;
  Sun 11 am- 8:30 pm

5822 Fairmont Parkway, Pasadena, TX 77505   281-991-5645
  Hours: M-Th 10:30 am-9:30 pm; F 10:30 am-9:30 pm;
  Sat 10:30 am-9:30 pm; Sun 11am-8:30 PM

20220 Katy Freeway, Katy, TX 77449   281-599-3878
  Hours: M-Th 10:30 am-9:30 pm; F-Sat 10:30 am-10 pm;
  Sun 11 am- 8:30 pm

20030 US Hwy 59 N., Humble, TX 77338   281-548-1122
  Hours: M-Th 10:30 am-9:30 pm; F-Sat 10:30 am-10 pm;
  Sun 11 am- 8:30 pm

2715 Town Center Blvd., Sugar Land, TX 77479   281-980-5200
  Hours: M-Th 10:30 am-9:30 pm; F-Sat 10:30 am-10 pm;
  Sun 11 am- 8:30 pm
  www.SouperSalad.com

Kid Friendliness: B

Food Quality: B (freshness depends on the time of day though)
Price: $$

Spanish Flowers is another tasty Mexican food restaurant near downtown Houston. My daughter loved the fresh fruit platter as well as the chips and rice. The wait staff makes you want to come back for more. With hours like these, there's no excuse not to try it.

Physical location:

4701 North Main Street, Houston, TX 77009   713-869-1706
    Hours: Open 24 hours a day except from T at 10 pm-
    W at 9 am for cleaning

Kid Friendliness: B+
Food Quality: A
Price: $$

At **Sweet Tomatoes**, kids love being able to create their own meals. It's a good way to get your kids to eat salads and enjoy them. Sweet Tomatoes also has pasta, baked potatoes, pizza and wonderful soups. Don't forget the desserts, including muffins, Jell-O, fruit, ice cream, brownies and the special dessert of the month. How can you resist?

Physical locations:

8775 Katy Fwy., Houston, TX 77024   713-365-9594

17240 Tomball Pkwy., Houston, TX 77064   281-890-1133

12540 Sugardale Dr., Stafford, TX 77477   281-240-1400

1717 Lake Woodlands Dr., The Woodlands, TX 77380   281-292-0556
    www.SweetTomatoes.com

Hours: M-Th 11 am-9 pm; F-Sat 11 am-10 pm;
Sun 11 am-9 pm

Kid Friendliness: A-
Food: A
Price: $$

Turquoise is a Turkish restaurant recommended by a friend. She was right. It's delicious. The restaurant serves Mediterranean healthy food that's not too spicy. Best of all, the owner loves kids and is super friendly. When the restaurant isn't too busy (week nights), he will help your child make a pizza. We're not talking about playing with the dough. Your child becomes the chef and really makes his/her own pizza in the kitchen. Note: The restaurant can be hard to find because it functions as the deli for an office building.

Physical location:

3701 Kirby Drive near Richmond, TX 77098   713-526-3800
Hours: M-Th 8 am-9 pm; F 8 am-10 pm; Sat 11 am-11 pm;
Sun Noon-5 pm

Kid Friendliness: A+
Food: A
Price: $$

All of the **Willie's Restaurants** (Little Willie's, Willie's Icehouse, Fajita Willie's) have good food and a play area/sand box for the kids. Your family will like the hamburgers, fresh garden salads, homemade onion rings and much more.

Physical locations:

17492 Northwest Frwy., Houston, TX 77040   713-937-0456

4561 FM 1960 West, Houston, TX 77069 281-583-1151

7092 Highway 6 North, Houston, TX 77095 281-345-2090

19770 Tomball Parkway, Houston, TX 77070 281-477-6300

16846 I-45 North, Conroe, TX 77384 936-321-0065

945 Hwy. 6, Sugar Land, TX. 77478 281-242-2252

19905 Katy Frwy., Houston, TX 77094 281-492-6700

3481 East Sam Houston Pkwy. South, Pasadena, TX 77505 281-991-1400

14960 Northwest Frwy., Houston, TX 77040 713-466-7646

15650 FM 529, Houston, TX 77095 281-859-4700

www.WilliesRestaurants.com

Hours: M-Th 11 am-10 pm; F-Sat 11 am-11 pm; Sun 11 am-9:30 pm

Kid Friendliness: A

Food: B

Price: $$

INDEX 1: ALPHABETICAL LISTING OF ACTIVITIES

Activity	Page Number(s)

INDEX 2: ALPHABETICAL LISTING OF RESTAURANTS